THE CAVALIER POETS

THE
CAVALIER POETS

chosen and edited by

Robin Skelton

FABER AND FABER LTD

LONDON

933509

First published in 1970
by Faber and Faber Limited
*24 Russell Square London WC*1
Printed in Great Britain by
The Bowering Press Plymouth
All rights reserved

SBN: 571 09217 9

CONTENTS

CONTENTS

CONTENTS

INTRODUCTION

I

Only a few poets have escaped the attention of twentieth-century literary criticism, but among them are a number of the minor writers of the seventeenth century and especially those who flourished during the period 1625 to 1689. This is explicable partly in terms of the more obvious attractiveness of the Renaissance and Jacobean periods, and partly in terms of the appeal of the great writers of the time. It is also, perhaps, due to a general critical tendency in the years since Grierson produced his seminal edition of Donne in 1912 to divide mid-seventeenth-century poetry into the Metaphysicals and the Others. Among the Others are, of course, several important figures such as Milton and Dryden, but Dryden has been associated with the work of his successors rather than his forebears and contemporaries, and Milton has remained in a lonely eminence.

Of the minor writers of the time few have suffered more than the Cavaliers. Dismissed by Pope as that 'mob of gentlemen that writ with ease' they have been regarded in general as amateur versifiers and entertainers undeserving the close critical and analytical attention demanded by the so-called metaphysicals. Thus, while the literature on George Herbert, Henry Vaughan, Thomas Traherne, Henry King, and Andrew Marvell is extensive, there is little adequate criticism of Carew, Suckling, Lovelace, Waller and their contemporaries and successors.

This lack of commentary has resulted in there being no truly adequate definition of 'Cavalier Poetry' and no established and generally accepted list of poets who can be reasonably grouped under this heading. In compiling this anthology, therefore, I have thought it necessary to re-examine the problem and attempt to define the characteristics and limits of what was, in my view, both a lively and historically important 'movement'.

II

The starting point of Cavalier Poetry was the work of Jonson and Donne. In the poems of the generally accepted Cavaliers—those Royalist poets who were involved in the troubles of the time of Charles I—we find characteristics derived clearly from both. Carew, a generally accepted leader of the mode, published his admiration of them, and in the works of both Lovelace and Suckling, Jonsonian classicism and wit rubs shoulders with Donnian vigour and the use of elaborate conceits. It was the Cavaliers' achievement to combine the strong points of both manners, and to provide a style of poetry that led directly onwards to the eighteenth century. It is to be noted that, while the eighteenth century was dubious of Donne, it was enthusiastic about the 'smoothness' of Waller, and found it possible to develop the sophisticated pastoralism of Lovelace and his followers, as well as the dry urbanity and poise of Carew, while it could not stomach the complexities of the metaphysicals.

It is, of course, usually the minor poetry of any period which lays the basis for the great poetry of the next, either by establishing and developing a manner which awaits another and later hand to develop its full potential, or by creating a conventional mediocrity which calls for attack and destruction. Dryden developed what the Cavaliers discovered; Wordsworth reacted against the flaccid poeticism and sterility of the minor Augustans; Browning developed the loose blank verse of the post-Romantics and Auden and his friends attacked Georgianism. In all these cases the emergence of new and vital poetry made it hard to see the virtues of the minor poetry which had preceded it.

So far it may appear that I have turned from a discussion of the Cavaliers to a discussion of all the minor poetry of the period between the accession of Charles I and the turn of the century. The term 'Cavaliers' has not, previously, been allowed to apply to other than a small group of writers, all of whom flourished in the reign of the first Charles. Once one begins to examine the poetry of these writers, however, and to place it alongside the poetry of their immediate successors it becomes apparent that what is most characteristic of the earlier is also most characteristic of the later writers of the period. There is continuity in both style and subject matter.

It would be best, perhaps, to start with a consideration of the word 'Cavalier' as applying to manner rather than subject matter, and to take as our examples two or three generally accepted members of the group.

The first thing one notes is that the Cavalier, as presented by both Carew and Suckling, is a man much engaged in the social round, and at once entertained and disquieted by the pleasures and frivolities of his culture. The love-songs of Carew and of Suckling reveal a wholehearted enjoyment of sexual pleasure and a disinclination to sentimentalize about it. Carew's *The Complement*, after praising the woman to the point of near absurdity suddenly tires of the conventional game, indulges in a moment of anti-climactic humour, and then displays a candid lust and affection which is all the more endearing for containing an element of self-mockery. The anti-Petrarchanism of Donne finds an echo in Suckling's dismissal of a too coy mistress, and in his description of the battle of the sexes in terms of a siege. The Chloes and Strephons of the Cavaliers are resistant to the notion of mere sighs and tears and, while there are charming pastoral poems in Lovelace, they are elaborate and sophisticated games rather than instances of true nostalgia. When a Cavalier echoes or imitates Marlowe's passionate shepherd, he is likely to hint at the inadequacies of mere idealism, and even wickedly to parody his original.

Nevertheless, the capacity for self-mockery, for scepticism, is combined, frequently, with a moral directness destructive of sententiousness yet productive of dignity. It is interesting to note that Lovelace's epigrammatic and cleanly phrased conclusions to his two best known poems find stylistic echoes in many other poets of the period. These conclusions are often neatly antithetical, and sum up a moral or emotional conflict displayed in the preceding lines. Lovelace writes,

23

'I could not love thee deare so much
Loved I not honour more.'

Similarly Sir Robert Howard ends his poem *To the Unconstant Cynthia*

'Yet we may love, but on this diff'rent score,
You what I am, I what you were before.'

Other examples are easy to find, and some of these are deliberate echoes. Tom d'Urfey ends another Cynthia poem

'Not to my Virtue, but thy Power,
This Constancy is due;
When change it self can give no more,
'Tis easie to be true.'

Sir George Etherege sums up his feelings in *The Rival* with

'How great so e'er your rigors are,
With them alone I'll cope;
I can endure my own despair
But not another's hope.'

Another stylistic device which runs through the century is the use of the catalogue of epithets which finally becoming absurd is suddenly countered by a moment of candour. This device, used beautifully by Donne in *Love's Progress* and Carew in *The Complement*, is used with greater subtlety by Marvell in *To His Coy Mistress*, and less exhaustively by Sir Aston Cokayne.

The amorous and erotic verse of the century is one of its finest achievements. It is clear that Jonson provided the hint with his three or four lucid, yet wry love songs, and that Donne provided a further hint with his *Goe and Catche a Falling Starre*. Eroticism, however, was far from being the Cavaliers' only theme. It was simply a part of their presentation of man as extrovert rather than introvert, as a social rather than as a solitary creature. Another aspect of the Cavalier mode was, of course, its use of epistles and, in particular familiar epistles relating to themes of hospitality. The scurrilous letters of Etherege are derived, clearly, from Jonson's *Invitation to Supper*, and from many other intermediate works. Many of these are too chatty to rate as fine poetry, though they are often sociologically illuminating. Again, it is social man that is being presented, as he is also being presented in the numerous satires of the period, all of which owe a great deal to Jonson. Satires run to length, and, in any case, are so often written from the point of view of a detached and impersonal recorder that they do not fit well into this anthology. They may be characteristic of the period, but they are not, essentially, Cavalier, for they are public verse rather than (to make a perhaps fine distinction), social verse. They are written for an audience of other than friends; they establish the existence of a public conscience. The Cavalier man, the social man, is not a polemicist. He may well (like Montrose and others) allude to political events, or write epitaphs upon notable figures or compose wry elegies, but he does not pamphleteer. Indeed, the mode is a little suspicious of public fame; the epitaphs—such as that on the Earl of Strafford by John Cleveland, or on Lady Mary Villers by Thomas Carew, emphasize individual mortality rather than public loss. Finally the individual, however sociable he may be or have been, is alone.

Solitude is, predictably, another theme of the times, and the conflict between the desire for social and sexual pleasures and the impulse towards solitude fills many pages from 1625 to 1688. It may be partly the result of the fortunes of war that there are so many poems about the delights of rustication and the stupidity of even dreaming of returning to town. One remembers the fable of the fox and the grapes as one reads of the poets sent into the country by the Cromwellian triumph. These rustic poems, however, also derive from the Jonsonian tradition, and from a reaction against the fake pastoralism of earlier poetry. The Cavaliers, indeed, split rustic poetry off from pastoral poetry. The pastoral convention became largely used for themes of amorous encounter. The rustic, though not infrequently tinted with classical allusions, became a mode of reflecting upon man's need of simplicity, and solitude, and self-sufficiency. It was also, in part, the consequences of the fashionable man's search for new 'kicks', as well as a direct consequence of falling for the tone of Horace's 'Beatus ille qui procul', a poem which was much translated and varied upon during the period and, one must remember, also made use of by the young Alexander Pope for his *Ode on Solitude*.

The classics deeply affected the Cavaliers, but their favourite writers were not, it seems, Virgil (unless it were the Virgil of the Georgics) but Horace, Martial, and Anacreon. Martial was responsible for many of the Cavaliers' sallies and epigrams, as he was also responsible for some of Jonson's and Donne's. Many of the love lyrics remind one forcibly of the erotic epigrams in the Greek Anthology though, in all probability, the themes are taken from the popular Anacreon (Cowley translated him) rather than from Meleager, or Lucillius, or others of the wits of the decadence of Greek civilization.

Whereas the Horatian led to a calm and sober evaluation of simple rustic pleasures, and clearly affected Walton and Cotton as well as many others, there was also, in this period, an attempt at the naturalistic, though amusing, portrayal of peasant and rustic customs. Herrick's poems about Queen Mab and the rest of the fairies are well known. Others, however, joined him in singing their praises and indulged in much light-hearted fantasy that was not quite at one with the rest of the Cavalier persona, for its whimsicality was unadulterated by the sardonic, and its simplicity was qualified by a Spenserian indulgence in the grotesque. What was, however, characteristic was the commentary of the sophisticated man upon rustic goings-on. This received its first Cavalier treatment from Suckling in his *Ballad of a Wedding*, and there are several other Wedding Ballads in the period all of which owe more to Suckling than to Spenser, and all of which combine a note of spectatorial superiority with affection. Affection is not invariably present, however. William Browne's description of Lydford, though in the same witty, yet downright mode, is hardly a celebration. The sociable man has found rural society intolerable and is damned if he isn't going to say so and name names to boot.

Such outbursts as these, along with many amusing lyrics and witty *jeux d'esprit*, have caused many critics to be a contemptuous of the Cavalier tradition as was Pope who, in point of fact, was indebted to it. It is easy to see that the taste-makers, the leaders of fashion, in later periods would naturally be disinclined to rate the movement highly, for it challenged vividly and amusingly so many of their more earnest convictions. The taste of the eighteenth century prized more sober models; though triviality and bawdiness kept breaking through, they were justified by references to Juvenal rather than to Rochester and to the Classics rather than to the Cavaliers. The nineteenth-century romantics could not be expected to share the Cavalier approach to sexuality, and do not appear to have seen the rustic poems as anything but charming irrelevances. The eighties and nineties brought a revival of interest. A. H. Bullen made his anthologies of Lyrics from Elizabethan and Restoration Song Books at that time but, again, it was an interest in the charming that excited his readers not a real belief in the literary stature of the material. There was a possibility between the wars that more attention would be paid to the tradition and, indeed, scholars did edit many texts at this time. The poets, however, remained aloof, though there are Cavalier touches in some work of the thirties and the gaiety of some of the contributors to *New Verse* has a Cavalier ring. Whether or not the movement can find a sympathetic chord in the sixties, I do not know, but, looking at the current popularity of John Betjeman, and observing the large number of recent translations of Martial, and the Greek Anthology, I feel there may be some hope.

What, however, is there to be gained from a study of this poetry, apart from pleasure? Is it anything more than a minor and usually enjoyable tradition? I think that there is something here. Firstly I suggest that the Cavaliers created a collective persona that represented the majority attitude of the educated leisured gentleman of the time, and if it sought to entertain with frivolity, it also, and simultaneously, sought the destruction of cant and sentiment and valued clarity of mind and heart. Secondly, the very 'amateur' pose of this persona enabled the poems to combine the discussion of minutiae with the presentation of strong personal convictions. Though often elegant and neat, the poems frequently include intimate asides, and humanizing touches of pathos and gaucherie. The persona, in fact, is rarely that of the adept, it is usually that of the raconteur rather than that of the authority; it can thus indulge in wayward fancy without jeopardizing its effectiveness; it can wink at us because it is never suggesting that man should be invariably devoted to high seriousness. In other words, the Cavaliers created a collective persona that could talk easily, charmingly, amusingly, bawdily, and sadly, and thus represent—more completely perhaps than most of the collective personae of succeeding literary movements—the whole range of the normal man's most usual sentiments and delights.

Many of the poems appear as if written, by sheer chance, in the middle of a crowded life devoted to other matters. Many of them, it seems, were in fact written that way, though the 'careless ease' of delivery should never blind us to the disciplined professionalism of such writers as Carew, or Rochester, or even the gaiety-loving Etherege and d'Urfey. This type of ease, however, enhances life by suggesting that it has primacy over literature; these poets support their sense of life with their verses—they do not see poetry as their *raison d'être*.

Such an attitude may seem shallow to us who make a fetish of a 'sense of vocation' and talk about a man's 'total commitment to the practice of his art'. It may also, however, serve to remind us that at a period when public events were overturning every established thing, when exile, civil war, revolution, and heresy were commonplaces of the time, the poets chose to reassert the primacy of the individual and the importance of ordinary human pleasure. Candid, witty, subtle, observant, sardonic, passionate, affectionate, and clear-headed, the poetry of the Cavaliers remains a monument to human dignity largely because it chose to avoid pretension while delighting equally in both simplicity and sophistication.

It is this approach which unifies the Lovelace-Suckling-Carew generation with the generation of Etherege-Rochester-Sedley-Dorset. The later group make more use of erotic themes and of the epistolary mode. They also indulge in satire which, as I have said, while sometimes involving the use of a Cavalier persona, more frequently implies a public status for the poet, which is at variance with the 'private gentleman' pose of the tradition as a whole. Nevertheless their membership of the Cavalier 'movement' is never seriously in doubt. In compiling this anthology, therefore, I have chosen to include appropriate poems from the reign of Charles II, rather than stick to those of the reign of his father. I could, of course, have gone further. Much of Prior is in the tradition, especially his lyrics, and there are good short poems by many of the early eighteenth-century writers. Nevertheless, when King Billy came to England, and when his reign gave way to that of Anne, the temper of poetry began to change. The moral directness of the Cavaliers had resulted in a candour which the new people found outrageous. Sentiment replaced candour, and the desire to instruct through delight replaced the desire simply to please. The pastoral tradition grew less amusing and more suited to the supposed tastes of the ladies. 'Ephelia' would one feels have been rather bored by the verse Addison recommended to his women readers, and Aphra Behn was certainly hardly likely to faint with shock at hearing a *risqué* joke, any more than did the ladies who admired Wycherley, Congreve, and the other Restoration Dramatists. When Steele and Farquhar took over the stage, however, things had changed.

It is not my business to discuss the change, only to indicate that by the accession of King Billy the Cavalier mode was almost finished, and that I have therefore taken the year of his coronation as the final date for this collection. All the poems in this book were first published in book form during the period 1625–1689 or, if published later, were probably written during the period. The oldest poet represented is Aurelian Townshend who was born in 1583, but whose work appeared during our period. The other poets born before the turn of the century are Sir Francis Kynaston (1587), William Browne (1592), Henry King (1592), Robert Herrick (1591), and Thomas Carew (1595). The works of all these writers first appeared after the coronation of Charles I. Of the other poets included all can be said to have reached their maturity during the Caroline, Cromwellian, or Restoration periods. In making my text I have, wherever possible, used the authoritative editions of recent scholars; where these did not exist I have returned to the original sources or accepted the versions presented in collections edited by established authorities in the field. I have most usually retained the original spelling, only modifying it a little to remove the u-v confusion to be found in some instances. It has not been my intention to create an 'authoritative' text, but to provide one reliable enough for use by the student and the general reader. I have been assisted in my work by a Research Grant from the University of Victoria.

ROBIN SKELTON

PHILIP AYRES

The Fly

Out of the wine-pot cried the Fly,
Whilst the grave Frog sat croaking by:
Than live a wat'ry life like thine,
I'd rather choose to die in wine.

I never water could endure,
Though ne'er so crystalline and pure.
Water's a murmurer, and they
Design more mischief than they say,
Where rivers smoothest are and clear,
Oh there's the danger, there's the fear;
But I'll not grieve to die in wine,
That name is sweet, that sound's divine.
    Thus from the wine-pot . . .

Dull fish in water live, we know,
And such insipid souls as thou;
While to the wine do nimbly fly,
Many such pretty birds as I:
With wine refreshed, as flowers with rain,
My blood is cleared, inspired my brain;
That when the Tory boys do sing,
I buzz i' th' chorus for the king.
    Thus from the wine-pot . . .

I'm more beloved than thou canst be,
Most creatures shun thy company;
I go unbid to every feast,
Nor stay for grace, but fall o' th' best:
There while I quaff in choicest wine,
Thou dost with puddle-water dine,

Which makes thee such a croaking thing.
Learn to drink wine, thou fool, and sing.
   Thus from the wine-pot . . .

In gardens I delight to stray,
And round the plants to sing and play:
Thy tune no mortal does avail,
Thou art the Dutchman's nightingale:
Would'st thou with wine but wet thy throat,
Sure thou would'st leave that dismal note;
Lewd water spoils thy organs quite,
And wine alone can set them right.
   Thus from the wine-pot . . .

Thy comrades still are newts and frogs,
Thy dwelling saw-pits, holes and bogs:
In cities I, and courts am free,
An insect too of quality.
What pleasures, ah! didst thou but know,
This heav'nly liquor can bestow:
To drink and drown thou'dst ne'er repine;
The great Anacreon died by wine.

   Out of the wine-pot cried the Fly,
   Whilst the grave Frog sat croaking by:
   Than live a wat'ry life like thine,
   I'd rather choose to die in wine.

THOMAS BEEDOME

To His Mistresse on Her Scorne

Resolve me, dearest, why two hearts in one
Should know the sinne of separation.
Must the sweete custome of our oft stolne kisses
Be lost, and we live empty of those blisses?
Or do the frownes of some old over-seer
Nourish thy feare, or make thy love lesse freer?
Why did'st thou suffer mee those sweetes to steale,
Which but thine own, no tongue can e're reveale,
And prompt mee to a daring, to beleeve
That my sad heart should find no cause to grieve,
Yet now at last hast mockt my hope so farre,
That I have met a cloud, though meant a starre?
Well, take thy tryumph, study but to be
True to thy selfe, as thou art false to mee,
And thou shalt meet a conquest yet. When I
Have groan'd unto the world my Elegy
And thy unjust disdaine, perhaps I shall
Obtaine this honour in my funerall:
Thy poysonous guilt, mixt with thy perjur'd breath,
May make thee wither with mee unto death:
So shall I tryumph in my Ashes too,
In that my innocence hath conquer'd you,
And then my eye rejoyce, in that I have
Thy scorne, to be a mourner at my grave.

The Choyce

What care I though she be faire,—
Haire, snow-like hand, or Sun-like eye,

If in that beauty I not share,
Were she deformed, what care I?
What care I though she be foule,—
Haire, swarthy hand, or sunne-burnt eye,
So long as I enjoy her soule,
Let her be so, why, what care I?
Dimme sight is cosen'd with a glosse
Of gaudy gowne, or humerous haire;
Such gold in melting leave more drosse
Than some unpolish't pieces share.
Be she faire, or foule, or either,
Or made up of both together,
Be her heart mine, her hand or eye
Be what it will, why, what care I?

APHRA BEHN

Song.   Love Arm'd

Love in Fantastique Triumph satt,
Whilst Bleeding Hearts around him flow'd,
For whom Fresh paines he did Create,
And strange Tyranick power he show'd;
From thy Bright Eyes he took his fire,
Which round about, in sport he hurl'd;
But 'twas from mine he took desire,
Enough to undo the Amorous World.

From me he took his sighs and tears,
From thee his Pride and Crueltie;
From me his Languishments and Feares,
And every Killing Dart from thee;
Thus thou and I, the God have arm'd,
And set him up a Deity;
But my poor Heart alone is harm'd,
Whilst thine the Victor is, and free.

A Thousand Martyrs I Have Made

A thousand martyrs I have made,
    All sacrificed to my desire;
A thousand beauties have betray'd,
    That languish in resistless fire.
The untam'd heart to hand I brought,
And fixed the wild and wandering thought.

I never vow'd nor sigh'd in vain,
    But both, tho' false, were well received.

The fair are pleased to give us pain,
   And what they wish is soon believed.
And tho' I talk'd of wounds and smart,
Love's pleasures only touched my heart.

Alone the glory and the spoil
   I always laughing bore away;
The triumphs, without pain or toil,
   Without the hell, the heav'n of joy.
And while I thus at random rove
Despise the fools that whine for love.

ALEXANDER BROME

To His Friend J. H.

If thou canst fashion no excuse,
To stay at home, as 'tis thy use,
   When I do send for Thee.
Let neither sickness, way, nor rain,
With fond delusions thee detain,
   But come thy way to me.

Hang such a sickness, that has power,
To seize on thee at such an hour,
   When thou should'st take thy pleasure:
Go give thy Doctor half a Fee,
That it may never trouble thee,
   Until thou art at leisure.

We have a Cup of Cider here,
That scorns that Common strumpet, Beer,
   And such dull drinks as they're.
Their potions made of Hops and Malt,
Can only make our fancies halt,
   This makes them quick as air.

Ceres with Bacchus dares compare,
And swears her fruits the liquor are,
   That poets so implore:
A sip of Sack may work a verse,
But he that drinks a bowl of Her's,
   Shall thunder out a score.

To-morrow morning come away,
Friday we'll vote a happy day,
   In spite of Erra Pater:

And bring with you a spark or twain,
Such as will drink, and drink again,
  To treat about the matter.

The Resolve

Tell me not of a face that's fair,
  Nor lip and cheek that's red,
Nor of the tresses of her hair,
  Nor curls in order laid;
Nor of a rare seraphic voice,
  That like an Angel sings;
Though if I were to take my choice,
  I would have all these things:
But if thou wilt have me love
  And it must be a she,
The only argument can move
  Is, that she will love me.

The glories of your Ladies be
  But Metaphors of things;
And but resemble what we see
  Each common object brings.
Roses out-red their lips and cheeks,
  Lilies their whiteness stain:
What fool is he that shadows seeks
  And may the substance gain?
Then if thou'lt have me love a Lass,
  Let it be one that's kind,
Else I'm a servant to the glass,
  That's with Canary lin'd.

The Counsel

Why's my friend so melancholy?
    Prithee why so sad, why so sad?
Beauty's vain, and Love's a folly,
    Wealth and Women make men mad,
To him that has a heart that's jolly
    Nothing's grievous, nothing's sad.
          Come, cheer up my lad.

Does thy Mistress seem to fly thee?
    Prithee don't repine, don't repine:
If at first she does deny thee
    Of her love, deny her thine;
She shows her coyness but to try thee,
    And will triumph if thou pine.
          Drown thy thoughts in wine.

Try again, and don't give over,
    Ply her, she's thine own, she's thine own;
Cowardice undoes a Lover.
    They are Tyrants if you moan;
If nor thyself, nor love can move her,
    But she'll slight thee and be gone:
          Let her then alone.

If thy Courtship can't invite her,
    Nor to condescend, nor to bend;
Thy only wisdom is to slight her,
    And her beauty discommend.
Such a niceness will requite her;
    Yet if thy love will not end,
          Love thyself and friend.

The Contrary

Nay, prithee do, be coy and slight me,
　　I must love, though thou abhor it;
This pretty niceness does invite me:
　　Scorn me, and I'll love thee for it.
That World of beauty that is in you,
　　I'll overcome like Alexander.
In amorous flames I can continue
　　Unsing'd, and prove a Salamander.

Do not be won too soon I prithee,
　　But let me woo, whilst thou dost fly me.
'Tis my delight to dally with thee,
　　I'll court thee still if thou'lt deny me;
For there's no happiness but loving,
　　Enjoyment makes our pleasures flat;
Give me the heart that's always moving,
　　And's not confin'd t' one, you know what.

I've fresh supplies on all occasions,
　　Of thoughts, as various as your face is,
No Directory for evasions,
　　Nor will I court by common-places.
My heart's with Antidotes provided,
　　Nor will I die 'cause you frown on me;
I'm merry when I am derided,
　　When you laugh at me, or upon me.

'Tis fancy that creates those pleasures
　　That have no being but conceited;
And when we come to dig those treasures,
　　We see ourselves ourselves have cheated:
But if thou'rt minded to destroy me,
　　Then love me much, and love me ever,
I'll love thee more, and that may slay me,
　　So I thy Martyr am, or never.

Courtship

My Lesbia, let us live and love,
  Let crabbed Age talk what it will.
The Sun when down, returns above,
  But we, once dead, must be so still.

Kiss me a thousand times, and then
  Give me a hundred kisses more,
Now kiss a thousand times again,
  Then t'other hundred as before.

Come, a third thousand, and to those
  Another hundred kisses fix;
That done, to make the sweeter close,
  We'll millions of kisses mix.

And huddle them together so,
  That we ourselves shan't know how many,
And others can't their number know,
  If we should envy'd be by any.

And then, when we have done all this,
  That our pleasures may remain,
We'll continue on our bliss,
  By unkissing all again.

Thus we'll love, and thus we'll live,
  While our posting minutes fly,
We'll have no time to vex or grieve,
  But kiss and unkiss till we die.

The Royalist

Come, pass about the bowl to me,
    A health to our distressed king;
Though we're in hold, let cups go free,
    Birds in a cage may freely sing.
The ground does tipple healths apace,
    When storms do fall, and shall not we?
A sorrow dares not show his face,
    When we are ships and sack's the sea.

Pox on this grief, hang wealth, let's sing,
    Shall's kill ourselves for fear of death?
We'll live by th' air which songs doth bring,
    Our sighing does but waste our breath:
Then let us not be discontent,
    Nor drink a glass the less of Wine;
In vain they'll think their plagues are spent,
    When once they see we don't repine.

We do not suffer here alone,
    Though we are beggar'd, so's the king;
'Tis sin t' have wealth, when he has none,
    Tush! poverty's a royal thing!
When we are larded well with drink,
    Our heads shall turn as round as theirs,
Our feet shall rise, our bodies sink
    Clean down the wind, like Cavaliers.

Fill this unnatural quart with sack;
    Nature all vacuums doth decline,
Our selves will be a Zodiac,
    And every mouth shall be a sign.
Methinks the Travels of the glass,
    Are circular like Plato's year,
Where every thing is as it was;
    Let's tipple round; and so 'tis here.

To a Painted Lady

Leave these deluding tricks and shows,
    Be honest and downright:
What Nature did to view expose,
    Don't you keep out of sight.
The novice youth may chance admire
    Your dressings, paints and spells:
But we that are expert desire
    Your sex for somewhat else.

In your adored face and hair,
    What virtue could you find,
If Women were like Angels fair,
    And every man were blind?
You need no pains or time to waste
    To set your beauties forth,
With oils, and paint and drugs, that cost
    More than the face is worth.

Nature her self, her own work does
    And hates all needless arts,
And all your artificial shows
    Disgrace your Nat'ral parts.
You're flesh and blood and so are we,
    Let flesh and blood alone,
To love all compounds hateful be,
    Give me the pure, or none.

The Anti-Politician

Come leave thy care, and love thy friend;
　　Live freely, don't despair,
Of getting money there's no end,
　　And keeping it breeds care.
If thou hast money at thy need,
　　Good company, and good Wine,
His life, whose joys on wealth do feed,
　　's not half so sweet as thine.

I can enjoy myself and friends,
　　Without design or fear,
Below their envy, or base ends,
　　That Politicians are.
I neither toil, nor care, nor grieve,
　　To gather, keep, or lose;
With freedom and content I live,
　　And what's my own I use.

While men blown on with strong desires
　　Of riches or renown,
Though ne'er so high, would still be higher,
　　So tumble headlong down.
For Princes' smiles turn oft to frowns,
　　And favours fade each hour;
He that to day heaps Towns on Towns,
　　To morrow's clapp'd i' th' Tower.

All that we get by all our store,
　　's but honour or dominion;
The one's but trouble varnish'd o'er,
　　And t'other's but opinion.
Fate rules the roost, Times always change;
　　'Tis fancy builds all things;
How madly then our minds do range,
　　Since all we grasp hath wings.

Those empty terms of rich and poor,
   Comparison hath fram'd;
He hath not much that covets more,
   Want is but will, nicknam'd.
If I can safely think and live,
   And freely laugh or sing,
My wealth I'll not for Crœsus give,
   Nor change lives with a King.

WILLIAM BROWNE

(Love Who Will, for I'll Love None)

Love who will, for I'll love none,
   There's fools enough beside me:
Yet if each woman have not one,
   Come to me where I hide me,
And if she can the place attain,
For once I'll be her fool again.

It is an easy place to find,
   And women sure should know it;
Yet thither serves not every wind,
   Nor many men can show it:
It is the storehouse, where doth lie
All women's truth and constancy.

If the journey be so long,
   No woman will adventer;
But dreading her weak vessel's wrong,
   The voyage will not enter:
Then may she sigh and lie alone,
In love with all, yet lov'd of none.

(Welcome, Welcome, do I Sing)

Welcome, welcome, do I sing,
Far more welcome than the spring;
He that parteth from you never
Shall enjoy a spring for ever.

He that to the voice is near
   Breaking from your iv'ry pale,

Need not walk abroad to hear
    The delightful nightingale.

Welcome, welcome, then I sing,
Far more welcome than the spring;
He that parteth from you never
Shall enjoy a spring for ever.

He that looks still on your eyes,
    Though the winter have begun
To benumb our arteries,
    Shall not want the summer's sun.
        Welcome, welcome, then I sing, &c.

He that still may see your cheeks,
    Where all rareness still reposes,
Is a fool, if e'er he seeks
    Other lilies, other roses,
        Welcome, welcome, &c.

He to whom your soft lip yields,
    And perceives your breath in kissing,
All the odours of the fields
    Never, never shall be missing.
        Welcome, welcome, &c.

He that question would anew
    What fair Eden was of old,
Let him rightly study you,
    And a brief of that behold.
        Welcome, welcome, then I, &c.

On the Countess Dowager of Pembroke

Underneath this sable herse
Lies the subject of all verse:
Sidney's sister, Pembroke's mother:

Death, ere thou hast slain another,
Fair, and learn'd, and good as she,
Time shall throw a dart at thee.

Marble piles let no man raise
To her name: for after days
Some kind woman born as she,
Reading this, like Niobe
Shall turn marble, and become
Both her mourner and her tomb.

On a Rope Maker Hanged

Here lies a man much wronged in his hopes,
Who got his wealth backwards by making of ropes.
It was his hard chance in his fortunes to falter,
For he liv'd by the rope, and died by the halter.

Lydford Journey

I oft have heard of Lydford law,
How in the morn they hang and draw,
    And sit in judgment after:
At first I wonder'd at it much;
But now I find their reason such,
    That it deserves no laughter.

They have a castle on a hill;
I took it for an old windmill,
    The vanes blown off by weather;
Than lie therein one night, 'tis guess'd,
'Tis better to be ston'd or press'd,
    Or hang'd, now choose you whether.

Ten men less room within this cave
Than five mice in a lanthorn have;
   The keepers they are sly ones:
If any could devise by art
To get it up into a cart,
   'Twere fit to carry lions.

When I beheld it, Lord! thought I,
What justice and what clemency
   Hath Lydford, when I spy all!
They know none there would gladly stay,
But rather hang out of the way,
   Than tarry for his trial.

The Prince a hundred pounds hath sent
To mend the leads and planchings rent
   Within this living tomb:
Some forty-five pounds more had paid
The debts of all that shall be laid
   There till the day of doom.

One lies there for a seam of malt,
Another for three pecks of salt,
   Two sureties for a noble;
If this be true, or else false news,
You may go ask of Mr. Crewes,
   John Vaughan, or John Doble.

Near to the men that lie in lurch,
There is a bridge, there is a church,
   Seven ashes, and an oak;
Three houses standing, and ten down;
They say the parson hath a gown,
   But I saw ne'er a cloak.

Whereby you may consider well,
That plain simplicity doth dwell
At Lydford without bravery;
For in that town, both young and grave
Do love the naked truth, and have
   No cloaks to hide their knavery.

This town's enclos'd with desert moors,
But where no bear nor lion roars,
   And nought can live but hogs:
For, all o'erturn'd by Noah's flood,
Of fourscore miles scarce one foot's good,
   And hills are wholly bogs.

And near hereto's the Gubbins' cave;
A people that no knowledge have
   Of law, or God, or men:
Whom Caesar never yet subdued;
Who've lawless liv'd; of manners rude:
   All savage in their den.

By whom,—if any pass that way,
He dares not the least time to stay,
   For presently they howl;
Upon which signal they do muster
Their naked forces in a cluster,
   Led forth by Roger Rowle.

The people all, within this clime,
Are frozen up all winter time;
   Be sure I do not fain;
And when the summer is begun
They lie like silkworms in the sun,
   And come to life again.

One told me, in King Caesar's time,
The town was built of stone and lime,
   But sure the walls were clay:
For they are fall'n, for ought I see,
And since the houses were got free,
   The town is run away.

O Caesar, if thou there didst reign,
Whilst one house stands, come there again;
   Come quickly, while there is one:
If thou but stay a little fit,
But five years more, they may commit
   The whole town into prison.

To see it thus much griev'd was I;
The proverb says, Sorrow is dry,
   So was I at this matter:
When by great chance, I know not how,
There thither came a strange stray'd cow,
   And we had milk and water.

Sure I believe it then did rain
A cow or two from Charles his wain,
   For none alive did see
Such kind of creatures there before,
Nor shall from hence for evermore,
   Save pris'ners, geese, and we.

To nine good stomachs, with our whig,
At last we got a tithing pig;
   This diet was our bounds:
And that was just as if 'twere known,
One pound of butter had been thrown
   Amongst a pack of hounds.

One glass of drink I got by chance,
'Twas claret when it was in France;
 But now from that nought wider:
I think a man might make as good
With green crabs boil'd with Brazil wood
 And half a pint of cider.

I kiss'd the Mayor's hand of the town,
Who, though he wear no scarlet gown,
 Honours the Rose and Thistle:
A piece of coral to the mace,
Which there I saw to serve the place,
 Would make a good child's whistle.

At six o' clock I came away,
And pray'd for those that were to stay,
 Within a place so arrant,
Wild and ope to winds that roar:
By God's grace I'll come there no more,
 Unless by some tin warrant.

GEORGE VILLIERS
DUKE OF BUCKINGHAM

To His Mistress

Phillis, though your all-powerful charms
Have forced me from my Celia's arms,
That sure defence against all powers
But those resistless eyes of yours,
Think not your conquest to maintain
By rigour or unjust disdain;
In vain, fair nymph, in vain you strive,
Since love does seldom hope survive:
Or if I languish for a time,
While all your glories in their prime
May justify such cruelty
By the same force that conquered me;
When age shall come, at whose command
Those troops of beauties must disband,
A tyrant's strength once too away,
What slave so dull as to obey?
These threatening dangers then remove:
Make me at least believe you love;
Dissemble, and by that sly art
Preserve and govern well my heart;
Of if you'll learn a nobler way
To keep your empire from decay,
And here for ever fix your throne,
Be kind, but kind to me alone.

JOHN BUNYAN

The Song of the Shepherd in the Valley of Humiliation

He that is down, needs fear no fall,
He that is low, no Pride:
He that is humble, ever shall
Have God to be his Guide.

I am content with what I have,
Little be it, or much:
And, Lord, Contentment still I crave,
Because thou savest such.

Fulness to such a burden is
That go on Pilgrimage:
Here little, and hereafter Bliss,
Is best from Age to Age.

THOMAS CAREW

The Spring

Now that the winter's gone, the earth hath lost
Her snow-white robes, and now no more the frost
Candies the grass, or castes an ycie creame
Upon the silver Lake, or Chrystall streame:
But the warme Sunne thawes the Benummed Earth,
And makes it tender, gives a sacred birth
To the dead Swallow; wakes in hollow tree
The drowzie Cuckow, and the Humble-Bee.
Now doe a quire of chirping Minstrels bring
In tryumph to the world, the youthfull Spring.
The Vallies, hills, and woods, in rich arraye,
Welcome the comming of the long'd for May.
Now all things smile; onely my *Love* doth lowre:
Nor hath the scalding Noon-day Sunne the power,
To melt that marble yce, which still doth hold
Her heart congeald, and makes her pittie cold.
The Oxe which lately did for shelter flie
Into the stall, doth now securely lie
In open fields; and love no more is made
By the fire side; but in the cooler shade
Amyntas now doth with his *Cloris* sleepe
Under a Sycamoure, and all things keepe
Time with the season, only shee doth carry
June in her eyes, in her heart *January*.

The Protestation, A Sonnet

No more shall meads be deckt with flowers,
Nor sweetnesse dwell in rosie bowers:

Nor greenest buds on branches spring,
Nor warbling birds delight to sing,
Nor Aprill violets paint the grove,
If I forsake my *Celias* love.

The fish shall in the Ocean burne,
And fountaines sweet shall bitter turne,
The humble oak no flood shall know,
When floods shall highest hills ore-flow;
Blacke *Laethe* shall oblivion leave,
If ere my *Celia* I deceive.

Love shall his bow and shaft lay by,
And *Venus* doves want wings to flie:
The Sun refuse to shew his light,
And day shall then be turn'd to night,
And in that night no starre appeare,
If once I leave my *Celia* deere.

Love shall no more inhabite earth,
Nor lovers more shall love for worth,
Nor joy above in heaven dwell,
Nor paine torment poore soules in hell;
Grim death no more shall horrid prove,
If ere I leave bright *Celias* love.

Good Counsel to a Young Maid
Song

Gaze not on thy beauties pride,
Tender Maid, in the false tide,
That from Lovers eyes doth slide.

Let thy faithfull Crystall show,
How thy colours come, and goe:
Beautie takes a foyle from woe.

Love, that in those smooth streames lyes,
Under pitties faire disguise,
Will thy melting heart surprize.

Netts, of passions finest thred,
Snaring Poems, will be spred,
All, to catch thy maiden-head.

Then beware, for those that cure
Loves disease, themselves endure
For reward, a Calenture.

Rather let the Lover pine,
Then his pale cheeke, should assigne
A perpetuall blush to thine.

Song
To My Inconstant Mistris

When thou, poore excommunicate
  From all the joyes of love, shalt see
The full reward, and glorious fate,
  Which my strong faith shall purchase me,
  Then curse thine owne inconstancie.

A fayrer hand then thine, shall cure
  That heart, which thy false oathes did wound;
And to my soul, a soul more pure
  Than thine, shall by Loves hand be bound,
  And both with equall glory crown'd.

Then shalt thou weepe, entreat, complaine
   To Love, as I did once to thee;
When all thy teares shall be as vaine
   As mine were then, for thou shalt bee
Damn'd for thy false Apostasie.

A Deposition from Love

I was foretold, your rebell sex,
   Nor love, nor pitty knew;
And with what scorne, you use to vex
   Poore hearts, that humbly sue;
Yet I believ'd, to crowne our paine,
   Could we the fortresse win,
The happy lover sure should gaine
   A Paradise within:
I thought loves plagues, like Dragons sate,
Only to fright us at the gate.

But I did enter, and enjoy,
   What happy lovers prove;
For I could kisse, and sport, and toy,
   And tast those sweets of love;
Which had they but a lasting state,
   Or if in *Celia's* brest,
The force of love might not abate,
   Jove were too mean a guest.
But now her breach of faith, far more
Afflicts, then did her scorne before.

Hard fate! to have been once possest
   As victor, of a heart,
Atchiev'd with labour, and unrest,
   And then forc'd to depart.

If the stout Foe will not resigne,
   When I besiege a Towne,
I lose, but what was never mine;
   But he that is cast downe
From enjoy'd beautie, feeles a woe,
Onely deposed Kings can know.

Disdaine Returned

Hee that loves a Rosie cheeke,
   Or a corall lip admires,
Or from star-like eyes doth seeke
   Fuell to maintaine his fires;
As old *Time* makes these decay,
So his flames must waste away.

But smooth, and stedfast mind,
   Gentle thoughts, and calme desires,
Hearts, with equall love combind,
   Kindle never dying fires.
Where these are not, I despise
Lovely cheekes, or lips, or eyes.

No teares, *Celia*, now shall win,
   My resolv'd heart, to returne;
I have searcht thy soule within,
   And find nought, but pride, and scorne;
I have learn'd thy arts, and now
   Can disdaine as much as thou.
Some power, in my revenge convay
That love to her, I cast away.

A Pastorall Dialogue
Celia   Cleon

As Celia rested in the shade
    With *Cleon* by her side,
The swaine thus courted the young Maid,
    And thus the Nymph replide.

CL

Sweet! let thy captive, fetters weare
    Made of thine armes, and hands;
Till such as thraldome scorne, or feare,
    Envie those happy bands.

CE

Then thus my willing armes I winde
    About thee, and am so
Thy pris'ner; for my selfe I binde,
    Untill I let thee goe.

CL

Happy that slave, whom the faire foe
    Tyes in so soft a chaine.
CE Farre happier I, but that I know
    Thou wilt breake loose againe.

CL

    By thy immortall beauties never.
CE Fraile as thy love's thine oath.
CL Though beautie fade, my faith lasts ever.
CE Time will destroy them both.

CL

I dote not on thy snow-white skin.
CE What then? CL Thy purer mind.
CE It lov'd too soone. CL Thou hadst not bin
    So faire, if not so kind.

CE

Oh strange vaine fancie! CL But yet true.
CE Prove it. CL Then make a brade
Of those loose flames, that circle you,
    My sunnes, and yet your shade.

CE

'Tis done. CL Now give it me. CE Thus thou
    Shalt thine owne errour find,
If these were beauties, I am now
    Lesse faire, because more kind.

CL

You shall confesse you erre; that haire
    Shall it not change the hue,
Or leave the golden mountaine bare?
    CE Aye me! it is too true.

CL

But this small wreathe, shall ever stay
    In its first native prime,
And smiling when the rest decay,
    The triumphs sing of time.

CE

Then let me cut from thy faire grove,
    One branch, and let that be

An embleme of eternall love,
    For such is mine to thee.

CL

Thus are we both redeem'd from time,
    I by thy grace.   CE And I
Shall live in thy immortall rime,
    Untill the Muses dye.

CL

By heaven!   CE Sweare not; if I must weepe,
    Jove shall not smile at me;
This kisse, my heart, and thy faith keepe.
CL This breathes my soule to thee.

Then forth the thicket *Thirsis* rusht,
    Where he saw all their play:
The swaine stood still, and smil'd, and blusht,
    The Nymph fled fast away.

To a Lady that Desired I would Love Her

1

Now that you have freely given me leave to love,
    What will you doe?
    Shall I your mirth, or passion move
    When I begin to wooe;
Will you torment, or scorne, or love me too?

2

Each pettie beautie can disdaine, and I
    Spight of your hate

Without your leave can see, and dye;
Dispence a nobler Fate,
'Tis easie to destroy, you may create.

3

Then give me leave to love, and love me too,
Not with designe
To rayse, as Loves curst Rebells doe,
When puling Poets whine,
Fame to their beautie, from their blubbr'd eyne.

4

Griefe is a puddle, and reflects not clearee
Your beauties rayes,
Joyes are pure streames, your eyes appeare
Sullen in sadder layes,
In chearfull numbers they shine bright with prayse;

5

Which shall not mention to express you fayre
Wounds, flames, and darts,
Stormes in your brow, nets in your haire,
Suborning all your parts,
Or to betray, or torture captive hearts.

6

I'le make your eyes like morning Suns appeare,
As milde, and faire;
Your brow as Crystall smooth, and cleare,
And your dishevell'd hayre
Shall flow like a calme Region of the Ayre.

7

Rich Nature stores, (which is the Poets Treasure)
　　　I'le spend, to dresse
Your beauties, if your mine of Pleasure
　　　In equall thankfulnesse
You but unlocke, so we each other blesse.

The Comparison

Dearest thy tresses are not threads of gold,
Thy eyes of Diamonds, nor doe I hold
Thy lips for Rubies: Thy faire cheekes to be
Fresh Roses; or thy teeth of Ivorie:
Thy skin that doth thy daintie bodie sheath
Not Alabaster is, nor dost thou breath
Arabian odours, those the earth brings forth
Compar'd with which would impaire thy worth.
Such may be others Mistresses, but mine
Holds nothing earthly, but is all divine.
Thy tresses are those rayes that doe arise
Not from one Sunne, but two; such are thy eyes:
Thy lips congealed Nectar are, and such
As but a Deitie, there's none dare touch.
The perfect crimson that thy cheeke doth cloath
(But only that it farre exceeds them both)
Aurora's blush resembles, or that redd
That *Iris* struts in when her mantl's spred.
Thy teeth in white doe *Leda's* Swan exceede,
Thy skin's a heavenly and immortall weede,
And when thou breath'st, the winds are ready strait
To filch it from thee, and doe therefore wait
Close at thy lips, and snatching it from thence
Beare it to Heaven, where 'tis *Joves* frankincense.
Faire Goddesse, since thy feature makes thee one,

Yet be not such for these respects alone;
But as you are divine in outward view
So be within as faire, as good, as true.

A Song

Aske me no more where *Jove* bestowes,
When *June* is past, the fading rose:
For in your beauties orient deepe,
These flowers as in their causes, sleepe.

Aske me no more whether doth stray,
The golden Atomes of the day:
For in pure love heaven did prepare
Those powders to inrich your haire.

Aske me no more whether doth hast,
The Nightingale when May is past:
For in your sweet dividing throat
She winters and keepes warme her note.

Aske me no more where those starres light,
That downewards fall in dead of night:
For in your eyes they sit, and there,
Fixed become as in their sphere.

Aske me no more if East or West,
The Phenix builds her spicy nest:
For unto you at last shee flies,
And in your fragrant bosome dyes.

The Complement

O my deerest I shall grieve thee
When I sweare, yet sweete beleeve me,
By thine eyes the tempting booke
On which even crabbed old men looke
I sweare to thee, (though none abhorre them)
Yet I doe not love thee for them.

I doe not love thee for that faire,
Rich fanne of thy most curious haire;
Thou the wires thereof be drawne
Finer then the threeds of lawne,
And are softer then the leaves
On which the subtle spinner weaves.

I doe not love thee for those flowers,
Growing on thy cheeks (loves bowers)
Though such cunning them hath spread
None can parte their white and red:
Loves golden arrowes thence are shot,
Yet for them I love thee not.

I doe not love thee for those soft,
Red corrall lips I've kist so oft;
Nor teeth of pearle, the double guard
To speech, whence musicke still is heard:
Though from those lips a kisse being taken,
Might tyrants melt and death awaken.

I doe not love thee (O my fairest)
For that richest, for that rarest
Silver pillar which stands under
Thy round head, that globe of wonder;
Though that necke be whiter farre,
Then towers of polisht Ivory are.

I doe not love thee for those mountaine
Hill'd with snow, whence milkey fountaines,
(Suger'd sweete, as sirropt berries)
Must one day run through pipes of cherries;
O how much those breasts doe move me,
Yet for them I doe not love thee:

I doe not love thee for that belly,
Sleeke as satten, soft as jelly,
Though within that Christall round
Heapes of treasure might be found,
So rich that for the least of them,
A King might leave his Diadem.

I doe not love thee for those thighes
Whose Alablaster rockes doe rise
So high and even that they stand
Like Sea-markes to some happy land.
Happy are those eyes have seene them,
More happy they that saile between them.

I love thee not for thy moist palme,
Though the dew thereof be balme:
Nor for thy pretty legge and foote,
Although it be the precious roote,
On which this goodly cedar growes,
(Sweete) I love thee not for those:

Nor for thy wit though pure and quicke,
Whose substance no arithmeticke
Can number downe: nor for those charmes
Mask't in thy embracing armes;
Though in them one night to lie,
Dearest I would gladly die.

I love not for those eyes, nor haire,
Nor cheekes, nor lips, nor teeth so rare;
Nor for thy speech, thy necke, nor breast,
Nor for thy belly, nor the rest:
Nor for thy hand, nor foote so small,
But wouldst thou know (deere sweet) for all.

A Rapture

I will enjoy thee now my *Celia*, come
   And flye with me to Loves Elizium:
The Gyant, Honour, that keepes cowards out,
Is but a Masquer, and the servile rout
Of baser subjects onely, bend in vaine
To the vast Idoll, whilst the nobler traine
Of valiant Lovers, daily sayle between
The huge Collosses legs, and passe unseene
Unto the blissfull shore; be bold, and wise,
And we shall enter, the grim Swisse denies
Only tame fooles a passage, that not know
He is but forme, and onely frights in show
The duller eyes that looke from farre; draw neere,
And thou shalt scorne, what we were wont to feare.
We shall see how the stalking Pageant goes
With borrowed legs, a heavie load to those
That made, and beare him; not as we once thought
The seeds of Gods, but a weake modell wrought
By greedy men, that seeke to enclose the common,
And within private armes empale free woman.
   Come then, and mounted on the wings of love
Wee'le cut the flitting ayre, and sore above
The Monsters head, and in the noblest seates
Of those blest shades, quench, and renew our heates.
There, shall the Queene of Love, and Innocence,

Beautie and Nature, banish all offence
From our close Ivy twines, there I'le behold
Thy bared snow, and thy unbraded gold.
There, my enfranchiz'd hand, on every side
Shall o're thy naked polish'd Ivory slide.
No curtaine there, though of transparent lawne,
Shall be before thy virgin-treasure drawne;
But the rich Mine, to the enquiring eye
Expos'd, shall ready still for mintage lye,
And we will coyne young *Cupids*. There, a bed
Of Roses, and fresh Myrtles, shall be spread
Under the cooler shade of Cypresse groves:
Our pillowes, of the downe of *Venus* Doves,
Whereon our panting lims wee'le gently lay
In the faint respites of our active play;
That so our slumbers, may in dreames have leisure,
To tell the nimble fancie our past pleasure;
And so our soules that cannot be ambrac'd,
Shall the embraces of our bodyes taste.
Meane while the bubbling streame shall court the shore,
Th' enamoured chirping Wood-quire shall adore
In varied tunes the Deitie of Love;
The gentle blasts of Westerne winds, shall move
The trembling leaves, & through their close bows breath
Still Musick, whilst we rest our selves beneath
Their dancing shade; till a soft murmure, sent
From soules entranc'd in amorous languishment
Rowze us, and shoot into our veins fresh fire,
Till we, in their sweet extasie expire.
    Then, as the empty Bee, that lately bore,
Into the common treasure, all her store,
Flyes 'bout the painted field with nimble wing,
Defloering the fresh virgins of the Spring;
So will I rifle all the sweets, that dwell
In my delicious Paradise, and swell
My bagge with honey, drawne forth by the power

Of fervent kisses, from each spicie flower.
I'le seize the Rose-buds in their perfum'd bed,
The Violet knots, like curious Mazes spread
O're all the Garden, taste the ripned Cherry,
The warme, firme Apple, tipt with corall berry:
Then will I visit, with a wandring kisse,
The vale of Lillies, and the Bower of blisse:
And where the beauteous Region doth divide
Into two milkie wayes, my lips shall slide
Fowne those smooth Allies, wearing as I goe
A tract for lovers on the printed snow;
Thence climbing o're the swelling *Appenine*,
Retire into thy grove of Eglantine;
Where I will all those ravisht sweets distill
Through Loves Alimbique and with Chimmique skill
From the mixt masse, one soveraigne Balme derive,
Then bring that great *Elixar* to thy hive.
    Now in more subtile wreathes I will entwine
My sonowie thighes, my legs and armes with thine;
Thou like a sea of milke shalt lye display'd,
Whilst I the smooth, calme Ocean, invade
With such a tempest, as when *Jove* of old
Fell downe on *Danae* in a storme of gold:
Yet my tall Pine, shall in the *Cyprian* straight
Ride safe at Anchor, and unlade her fraight:
My Rudder, with thy bold hand, like a tryde
And skilfull Pilot, thou shalt steere, and guide
My Bark into Loves channell, where it shall
Dance, as the bounding waves doe rise or fall:
Then shall thy circling armes, embrace and clip
My willing bodie, and thy balmie lip
Bathe me in juyce of kisses, whose perfume
Like a religious incense shall consume
And send up holy vapours, to those powres
That blesse our loves, and crowne our sportfull houres,
That with such Halcion calmeness, fix our soules

In steadfast peace, as no affright controules.
There, no rude sounds shake us with sudden starts,
No jealous eares, when we unrip our hearts
Sucke our discourse in, no observing spies
This blush, that glance traduce; no envious eyes
Watch our close meetings, nor are we betray'd
To Rivals, by the bribed chamber-maid.
No wedlock bonds unwreathe our twisted loves;
We seeke no midnight Arbor, no darke groves
To hide our kisses, there, the hated name
Of husband, wife, lust, modest, chaste, or shame,
Are vaine and empty words, whose very sound
Was never heard in the Elizian ground.
All things are lawfull there, that may delight
Nature, or unrestrained Appetite;
Like, and enjoy, to will, and act, is one,
We only sinne when Loves rotes are not done.
   The Roman *Lucrece* there, reades the divine
Lectures of Loves great master, *Aretif*,
And knowes as well as *Lais*, how to move
Her plyant body in the act of love.
To quench the burning Ravisher, she hurles
Her limbs into a thousand winding curles,
And studies artfull postures, such as be
Carv'd on the barke of every neighbouring tree
By learned hands, that so adorn'd the rinde
Of those faire Plants, which as they lay entwinde,
Have fann'd their glowing fires. The Grecian Dame,
That in her endlesse webb, toyl'd for a name
As fruitlesse as her worke, doth there display
Her self before the Youth of *Ithaca*,
And th'amorous sport of gamesome nights prefer,
Before dull dreames of the lost Traveller.
Daphne hath broke her barke, and that swift foot,
Which th'angry Gods had fastned with a root
To the fixt earth, doth now unfetter'd run,

To meet th'embraces of the youthfull Sun:
She hangs upon him, like his Delphique Lyre,
Her kisses blow the old, and breath new fire:
Full of her God, she sings inspired Layes,
Sweet Odes of love, such as deserve the Bayes,
Which she her selfe was. Next her, *Laura* lyes
In *Petrarchs* learned armes, drying those eyes
That did in such sweet smooth-pac'd numbers flow,
As made the world enamour'd of his woe.
These, and ten thousand Beauties more, that dy'de
Slave to the Tyrant, now enlarg'd, deride
His cancell'd lawes, and for their time mispent,
Pay into Loves Exchequer double rent.
   Come then my *Celia*, wee'le no more forbeare
To taste our joyes, struck with a Pannique feare,
But will depose from his imperious sway
This proud *Userper* and walke free, as they
With necks unyoak's; nor is it just that Hee
Should fetter your soft sex with Chastitie,
Which Nature made unapt for abstinence;
When yet this false Impostor can dispence
With humane Justice, and with sacred right,
And maugre both their lawes command me fight
With Rivals, or with emulous Loves, that dare
Equall with thine, their Mistresse eyes, or haire:
If thou complaine of wrong, and call my sword
To carve out thy revenge, upon that word
He bids me fight and kill, or else he brands
With markes of infamie my coward hands,
And yet religion bids from blood-shed flye,
And damns me for that Act. Then tell me why
This Goblin Honour which the world adores,
Should make men Atheists, and not women Whores.

Epitaph on the Lady Mary Villers

The Lady *Mary Villers* lyes
Under this stone; with weeping eyes
The Parents that first gave her birth,
And their sad Friends, lay'd her in earth:
If any of them (Reader) were
Knowne unto thee, shed a teare,
Or if thyselfe possesse a gemme,
As deare to thee, as this to them,
Though a stranger to this place,
Bewayle in theirs, thine owne hard case;
For thou perhaps at thy returne
Mayest find thy Darling in an Urne.

WILLIAM CARTWRIGHT

Lesbia on Her Sparrow

Tell me not of Joy: there's none
Now my little Sparrow's gone;
   He, just as you
   Would toy and wooe,
He would chirp and flatter me,
He would hang the Wing a while,
Till at length he saw me smile,
Lord how sullen he would be?

He would catch a Crumb, and then
Sporting let it go agen,
   He from my Lip
   Would moysture sip,
He would from my Trencher feed,
Then would hop, and then would run,
And cry *Philip* when h' had done,
O whose heart can choose but bleed?

O how eager would he fight?
And ne'er hurt though he did bite:
   No Morn did pass
   But on my Glass
He would sit, and mark, and do
What I did, now ruffle all
His Feathers o'r, now let 'em fall,
And then straightway sleek 'em too.

Whence will *Cupid* get his Darts
Feather'd now to peirce our hearts?
   A wound he may,
   Not Love conveigh,

Now this faithfull Bird is gone,
O let Mournfull Turtles joyn
With Loving Red-breasts, and combine
To sing Dirges o'r his Stone.

ROBERT CHAMBERLAIN

In Praise of Country Life

The winged fancies of the learned quill
Tell of strange wonders: sweet Parnassus' hill,
Castalia's well, the Heliconian spring,
Star-spangled valleys where the Muses sing.
Admired things another storie yeelds,
Of pleasant Tempe and th'Elysian fields;
Yet these are nothing to the sweet that dwells
In low-built cottages and country cells.
What are the scepters, thrones, and crownes of Kings,
But gilded burdens and most fickle things?
What are great offices but cumbring troubles?
And what are honours but dissolving bubbles?
What though the gates of greatness be frequented
With chains of glittering gold? He that's contented
Lives in a thousand times a happier way
Than he that's tended thus from day to day.
Matters of state, nor yet domestick jars,
Comets portending death, nor blazing stars,
Trouble his thoughts: hee'l not post-haste run on
Through Lethe, Styx, and fiery Phlegiton
For gold or silver: he will not affright
His golden slumbers in the silent night
For all the pretious wealth or sumptuous pride
That lies by Tiber, Nile, or Ganges' side.
Th'imbroider'd meadows, and the crawling streams
Make soft and sweet his undisturbed dreams.
He revels not by day nor in the nights,
Nor cares he much for musical delights:
And yet his humble roofe maintains a quire
Of singing crickets round about the fire.
This harmless life he leads—and, dare I say,
Doth neither wish, nor fear, his dying day.

SIR JAMES CHAMBERLAYNE

Dedication

1

This little Book, my God and King,
The first fruits of my Muse, I bring
Unto thy throne, an Offering.

2

'Twould look more lovely, I confess,
Were it attir'd in the dress
Of abler Pens, than in my Verse;

3

But since my Numbers could not flow
In loftier Strains, than here they do,
For Reasons Thou and I do know;

4

Accept the Present; though it be
Too mean a gift for Majesty,
Lord, 'tis my All, and due to Thee.

JOHN CLEVELAND

Epitaph on the Earl of Strafford

Here lies wise and valiant dust,
Huddled up 'twixt fit and juste:
Strafford, who was hurried hence
'Twixt treason and convenience.
He spent his time here in a mist,
A *Papist*, yet a *Calvinist*;
His Prince's nearest joy and Grief:
He had, yet wanted, all relief:
The Prop and Ruine of the State,
The peoples violent love and hate.
One in extremes lov'd and abhorr'd.
Riddles lie here, or in a word,
Here lies blood, and let it lie
Speechless still, and never cry.

SIR ASTON COKAYNE

To Plautia

Away, fond Thing! tempt me no more!
I'le not be won with all thy store!
I can behold thy golden hair,
And for the owner nothing care:
Thy Starry eyes can look upon,
And be mine own when I have done;
Thy cherry, ruby lips can kiss,
And for fruition never wish:
Can view the Garden of thy cheeks,
And slight the roses there as leeks:
Can hear thee sing with all thine Art,
Without enthralling of mine heart:
My Liberty thou can'st not wrong
With all the Magick of thy tongue:
Thy warm Snow-breasts and I can see
And neither sigh nor wish for thee:
Behold thy feet, which we do bless
For bearing so much happiness,
Yet they at all should not destroy
My strong-preserved Liberty:
Could see thee naked, as at first
Our Parents were, when both uncurst,
And with my busy, searching eyes
View strictly thy hid rarities;
Yet, after such a free survey,
From thee no Lover go away.
For thou art false and wilt be so:
I else no other fair would woo.
Away, therefore, tempt me no more!
I'le not be won with all thy store.

Of a Mistress

I love a lass as fair as ere was seen,
  Yet have I never seen if she be fair:
Grandees her suitors have and servants been
  And they that wooe her now great Nobles are;
How can I, therefore, think that she will deign
To look on me? I fear I love in vain.

Unto the Beauty which I do so desire
  I will make haste, to see how fair she is;
And though I find my betters wooers by her,
  I will be bold, and all my thoughts express;
Which when I have done, will she, therefore, deign
To pity me? I fear I love in vain.

I'le tell her that her hairs are golden Twines
  Able t'enamour all the Deities;
And that her eyes are two celestial signs,
  More glorious than the twelve within the skies.
When I have told her this, will she then deign
To love me too? I fear I love in vain.

If, (when that I have said what I can say
  And made what Protestations I can make),
She will be proud and coy, and say me Nay,
  Though ne'er so fair, my heart from her I'le take.
I will not subject be to her disdain:
The world shall never say I love in vain.

MATTHEW COPPINGER

A Song

I will not tell her that she's fair,
   For that she knows as well as I,
And that her Vertues equal are
   Unto the Glorys of her Eye.

And that I love her well she knows,
   For who can view that Heavenly Face,
Not paying that Respect he owes
   To Beauty bearing such a Grace?

But this I'le tell and tell her true:
   She takes upon her too much State;
For, by the Gods, it would undo
   A King to Love at such a rate!

Let Common Beauties boast the Power
   Of some uncommon Excellence,
And thank Dame Nature for the Dower
   Of that decoying, Charming Sense;

Adorn themselves with Pearls and Gold
   In Rubies and Rich Diamonds shine,
In choicest Silks that may be sold
   And all to make such Ladies Fine.

These are like some Rich Monument,
   Rais'd all of carv'd and costly Stones,
Painted and Gilt for Ornament;
   But full within of dead Men's Bones.

Such common ways my Clelia scorns,
   Her lovely Soul is too sublime;

She's not complete that Cloaths adorns,
  Or does in aught but Nature shine.

To Clelia

Coy Clelia, veil those Charming Eyes,
  From whose surprise there's none can part;
For he that gazes, surely dies,
  Or leaves behind a conquer'd Heart.

I durst not once presume to look,
  Or cast my wary Eyes aside:
But as a Boy that Cons his Book,
  Close sitting by his Master's side,

Dares not presume to look awry
  On Toys that catch the wandering sense;
So if I gaze I surely die:
  Against those Charms there's no defence.

Thus Heathens, at the Sun's up-rise,
  Unto the Ground did bow their Head,
Not able with their feeble Eyes
  To view their God they worshipped.

CHARLES COTTON

The Angler's Ballad

I

Away to the Brook,
All your Tackle out look,
   Here's a day that is worth a year's wishing;
See that all things be right,
For 'tis a very spight
   To want tools when a man goes a fishing.

II

Your Rod with tops two,
For the same will not doe
   If your manner of angling you vary
And full well you may think,
If you troll with a Pink,
   One too weak will be apt to miscarry.

III

Then Basket, neat made
By a Master in's trade,
   In a belt at your shoulders must dangle;
For none e'er was so vain
To wear this to disdain,
   Who a true Brother was of the Angle.

IV

Next, Pouch must not fail,
Stuff'd as full as a Mail,
   With Wax, Cruels, Silks, Hair, Furs and Feathers,

To make several Flies,
For the several Skies,
   That shall kill in despight of all weathers.

V

The Boxes and Books
For your Lines and your Hooks,
   And, though not for strict need notwithstanding,
Your Scissors, and your Hone
To adjust your points on,
   With a Net to be sure for your landing.

VI

All these things being on,
'Tis high time we were gone,
   Down, and upward, that all may have pleasure;
Till, here meeting at night,
We shall have the delight
   To discourse of our Fortunes at leisure.

VII

The day's not too bright,
And the wind hits us right,
   And all Nature does seem to invite us;
We have all things at will
For to second our skill,
   As they all did conspire to delight us.

VIII

Or stream now, or still,
A large Panier will fill,
   Trout and Grailing to rise are so willing;

I dare venture to say
'Twill be a bloudy day,
　　And we all shall be weary of killing.

IX

Away then, away,
We lose sport by delay,
　　But first leave all our sorrows behind us;
If misfortune doe come,
We are all gone from home,
　　And a fishing she never can find us.

X

The Angler is free
From the cares that degree
　　Finds it self with so often tormented;
And though we should slay
Each a hundred to-day,
　　'Tis a slaughter needs ne'er be repented.

XI

And though we display
All our Arts to betray
　　What were made for man's Pleasure and Diet;
Yet both Princes and States
May, for all our quaint Baits,
　　Rule themselves and their People in quiet.

XII

We scratch not our pates,
Nor repine at the Rates
　　Our Superiors impose on our living;

But do frankly submit,
Knowing they have more wit
   In demanding, than we have in giving.

XIII

Whilst quiet we sit
We conclude all things fit,
   Acquiescing with hearty submission;
For, though simple, we know
That soft murmurs will grow
   At the last into down-right Sedition.

XIV

We care not who says,
And intends it dispraise,
   That an Angler t'a Fool is next neighbour;
Let him prate, what care we,
We're as honest as he,
   And so let him take that for his Labour.

XV

We covet no Wealth
But the Blessing of Health,
   And that greater good Conscience within;
Such devotion we bring
To our God and our King,
   That from either no offers can win.

XVI

Whilst we sit and fish
We do pray as we wish,
   For long life to our King *James* the Second;

Honest Anglers then may,
Or they've very foul play,
   With the best of good Subjects be reckon'd.

Epitaph on Mr Robert Port

Here lies hee, whom the Tyrants rage
Snatcht in a venerable age;
And here with him entomb'd do lye
Honour, and Hospitalitie.

Epitaph on Mris Mary Draper

I

Reader, if thou cast thine eye
   On this weeping stone below:
Know, that under it doth lye
   One, that never man did know.

II

Yet of all men full well known
   By those beauties of her breast:
For, of all shee wanted none,
   When Death call'd her to her rest.

III

Then, the Ladies, if they wou'd
   Dye like her, kinde Reader, tell,
They must strive to be as good
   Alive; or 'tis impossible.

To Chloris

Ode

Farewell, my Sweete, untill I come,
  Improved in Merritt, for thy sake,
With Characters of honour Home,
  Such, as thou canst not then but take.

To Loyaltie my Love must bow,
  My Honour too calls to the feild,
Where, for a Ladyes buske, I now
  Must keene, and sturdy Iron weild.

Yet, when I rush into those Armes,
  Where Death, and Danger do combine,
I shall lesse subject be to Harmes,
  Than to those killing eyes of thyne.

Since I coulde live in thy disdaine,
  Thou art so far become my Fate,
That I by nothing can be slaine,
  Untill thy sentence speaks my date.

But, if I seeme to fall in Warre,
  T'excuse the Murder you committ,
Be to my Memorie just so farr,
  As in thy Heart t'acknoledge it;

That's all I aske; which thou must give
  To him that dying, takes a Pride
It is for thee; and would not live
  Sole Prince of all the world beside.

Ode

To Chloris

I

Fair and Cruel, still in vain
   Must I adore, still, still persevere
Languish still, and still complain,
   And yet a Med'cine for my Feaver
Never, never must obtain?

II

Chloris, how are you to blame,
   To him that dies to be so cruel
Not to stay my falling frame,
   Since your fair eyes do dart the fuel
That still nourishes my flame?

III

Shade those Glories of thine eye,
   Or let their Influence be milder,
Beauty, and disdain destroy
   Alike, and make our Passions wilder,
Either let me live or die.

IV

I have lov'd thee (let me see;
   Lord, how long a time of loving!)
Years no less than three times three,
   Still my flame and pain improving,
Yet still paid with cruelty.

V

What more wouldst thou have of me?
  Sure I've serv'd a pretty season,
And so prov'd my constancy,
That methinks it is but reason
Love or Death should set me free.

Ode

I

Was ever man of Nature's framing
  So given o'er to roving,
Who have been twenty years a taming,
By ways that are not worth the naming,
  And now must die of loving?

II

Hell take me if she been't so winning
  That now I love her mainly,
And though in jeast at the beginning,
Yet now I'd wond'rous fain be sinning,
  And so have told her plainly.

III

At which she cries I doe not love her,
  And tells me of her Honor;
Then have I no way to disprove her,
And my true passion to discover,
  But streight to fall upon her.

IV

Which done, forsooth, she talks of wedding,
 But what will that avail her?
For though I am old Dog at Bedding,
I'm yet a man of so much reading,
 That there I sure shall fail her.

V

No, hang me if I ever marry,
 Till Womankind grow stancher,
I do delight delights to vary
And love not in one Hulk to tarry,
 But only Trim and Launch her.

Ode

To Cupid

I

Fond Love, deliver up thy Bow,
I am becom more Love than thou;
I am wanton growne, and wild,
Much lesse a Man, and more a Child,
From Venus borne, of chaster kind,
A better Archer, though as blind.

II

Surrender without more adoe,
I am both King and Subject too,
I will command, but must obey,
I am the Hunter, and the Prey,
I vanquish, yet am over come,
And sentencing, receive my doom.

III

No springing Beauty scapes my dart,
And ev'ry ripe one wounds my heart;
Thus whilst I wound, I wounded am,
And, firing others, turne to flame,
To shew how farr Love can combine
The Mortal part with the Divine.

IV

Faith, quit thy Empire, and com downe,
That thou and I may share the Crowne,
I've try'de the worst thy Armes can doe.
Come then, and tast my power too,
Which (howsoere it may fall short)
Will doubtlesse prove the better sport.

V

Yet doe not; for in feild and towne,
The females are soe loving growne,
Soe kind, or else soe lustfull, wee
Can neither erre, though neither see;
Keepe then thy owne dominions, Lad,
Two Loves would make all women mad.

Laura Sleeping

Winds whisper gently whilst she sleeps,
    And fan her with your cooling wings;
Whilst she her drops of Beauty weeps,
    From pure, and yet unrivall'd Springs.

Glide over Beauties Field her Face,
 To kiss her Lip, and Cheek be bold,
But with a calm, and stealing pace;
 Neither too rude; nor yet too cold.

Play in her beams, and crisp her Hair,
 With such a gale, as wings soft *Love*
And with so sweet, so rich an Air,
 As breathes from the *Arabian* Grove.

A Breath as hush't as Lovers sigh;
 Or that unfolds the Morning door:
Sweet, as the Winds, that gently fly,
 To sweep the *Springs* enamell'd Floor.

Murmur soft *Musick* to her Dreams,
 That pure, and unpolluted run,
Like to the new-born Christal Streams,
 Under the bright enamour'd Sun.

But when she waking shall display
 Her light, retire within your bar,
Her Breath is life, her Eyes are day,
 And all Mankind her Creatures are.

Clepsydra

I

Why, let it run! who bids it stay?
 Let us the while be merry;
Time there in water creeps away,
 With us it posts in Sherry.

II

Time not employ'd 's empty sound,
    Nor did kind Heaven lend it,
But that the Glass should quick go round,
    And men in pleasure spend it.

III

Then set thy foot, brave Boy, to mine,
    Ply quick to cure our thinking;
An hour-glass in an hour of Wine
    Would be but lazy drinking.

IV

The man that snores the hour-glass out
    Is truly a time-waster,
But we, who troll this glass about,
    Make him to post it faster.

V

Yet though he flies so fast, some think,
    'Tis well known to the Sages,
He'll not refuse to stay and drink,
    And yet perform his stages.

VI

Time waits us whilst we crown the hearth,
    And dotes on Rubie Faces,
And knows that this Carier of mirth
    Will help to mend our paces:

VII

He stays with him that loves good time,
    And never does refuse it,

And only runs away from him
That knows not how to use it:

VIII

He only steals by without noise
From those in grief that waste it,
But lives with the mad roaring Boys
That husband it, and taste it.

IX

The moralist perhaps may prate
Of vertue from his reading,
'Tis all but stale and foisted chat
To men of better breeding.

X

Time, to define it, is the space
That men enjoy their being;
'Tis not the hour, but drinking glass,
Makes time and life agreeing.

XI

He wisely does oblige his fate
Does chearfully obey it,
And is of Fops the greatest that
By temp'rance thinks to stay it.

XII

Come, ply the Glass then quick about,
To titillate the Gullet,
Sobriety's no charm, I doubt,
Against a Cannon-Bullet.

Ode

I

Come, let us drink away the time,
A pox upon this pelting rhyme!
When wine's run high, wit's in the prime.

II

Drinke, and stout drinkers are true joies,
Odes, Sonnets, and such little toyes,
Are exercises fitt for Boyes.

III

Then to our Liquor let us sit,
Wine makes the Soul for action fit,
Who bears most drinke, has the most wit.

IV

The whineing Lover, that does place
His wonder in a painted face,
And wasts his substance in the chase,

V

Could not in Melancholie pine,
Had hee affections soe divine,
As once to fall in Love with wine.

VI

The Gods themselves their revells keepe,
And in pure Nectar tipple deep,
When slothful Mortalls are asleepe.

VII

They fudled once, for recreation,
In water, which by all relation,
Did cause Deucalion's inundation.

VIII

The spangled Globe, as it held most,
Their bowl, was with salt-water dos't,
The sun-burnt centre was the tost.

IX

In drinke, Apollo always chose
His darkest oracles to disclose,
'Twas wine gave him his Rubie nose.

X

The Gods then let us imitate,
Secure of Fortune, and of Fate,
Wine witt, and courage does create.

XI

Whoe dares not drink's a wretched wight;
Nor can I think that man dares fight
All day, that dares not drink all night.

XII

Fill up the Goblet, let it swim
In foam, that overlooks the brim,
Hee that drinks deepest, here's to him.

XIII

Sobrietie, and studie breeds
Suspition of our thoughts, and deeds;
The downright drunkard no man heeds.

XIV

Let mee have sack, tobacco store,
A drunken friend, a little whore,
Protectour, I will ask no more.

ABRAHAM COWLEY

The Epicure
After Anacreon

Fill the *Bowl* with rosie Wine,
Around our temples *Roses* twine,
And let us cheerfully awhile,
Like the *Wine* and Roses smile.
Crown'd with *Roses* we contemn
Gyge's wealthy *Diadem*.
To day is *Ours*; what do we fear?
To day is *Ours*; we have it here.
Let's treat it kindly, that it may
Wish at least, with us to stay.
Let's banish *Business*, banish *Sorrow*
To the *Gods* belongs *To morrow*.

The Frailty

1

I know 'tis *sordid*, and 'tis *low*;
   (All this as well as you I know)
Which I so hotly now pursue;
   (I know all this as well as you)
But whilst this cursed flesh I bear,
And all the *Weakness*, and the *Baseness* there,
Alas, alas, it will be always so.

2

In vain, exceedingly in vain
I rage sometimes, and bite my *Chain*;

For to what purpose do I bite
With Teeth which ne're will break it quite?
For if the chiefest *Christian Head*,
Was by this sturdy *Tyrant buffeted*,
What wonder is it, if *weak* I be *slain*?

Age
After Anacreon

Oft am I by the Women told,
Poor *Anacreon* thou grow'st old.
Look how thy hairs are falling all;
Poor *Anacreon* how they fall?
Whether I grow old or no,
By th'effects I do not know.
This I know without being told,
'Tis time to *Live* if I grow Old,
'Tis time short pleasures now to take,
Of little *Life* the best to make,
And manage *wisely* the *last stake*.

The Wish

Well then; I now do plainly see,
   This busie world and I shall ne'er agree;
The very *Honie* of all earthly joy
   Does of all meats the soonest *cloy*,
   And they (methinks) deserve my pity,
Who for it can endure the strings,
The *Crowd*, and *Buz*, and *Murmurings*
   Of this great *Hive*, the *City*.

Ah, yet, e'er I descend to th' Grave
May I a *small House*, and *large Garden* have!
And a *few Friends*, and *many Books*, both true,
    Both wise, and both delightful too!
    And since *Love* ne'er will from me flee,
A *Mistress* moderately fair,
And good as *Guardian-Angels* are,
    Only belov'd, and loving me!

Oh, *Fountains*, when in you shall I
My self, eas'd of unpeaceful thoughts, espy?
Oh *Fields!* Oh *Woods!* when, when shall I be made
    The happy Tenant of your shade?
    Here's the Spring-head of *Pleasures* flood;
Where all the *Riches* lie, that she
    Has coyn'd and stampt for good.

Pride and *Ambition* here,
Only in *far fetcht* Metaphors appear;
Here nought but *winds* can hurtful *Murmurs* scatter,
    And nought but *Eccho flatter*.
    The *Gods*, when they descended, hither
From Heav'en did always chuse their way;
And therefore we may boldly say,
    That 'tis the *way* too *thither*.

How happy here should I,
And one dear *She* live, and embracing dy?
She who is all the world, and can exclude
    In *desarts Solitude*.
    I should have then this for only fear,
Lest men, when they my pleasures see,
Should higher throng to live like me,
    And so make a *City* here.

Horat. Epodon.

Beatus ille qui procul, etc.

Happy the Man whom bount'ous Gods allow
With his own Hands Paternal Grounds to plough!
Like the first golden Mortals happy he
From Bus'ness and the cares of Money free!
No humane storms break off at Land his sleep
No loud Alarms of Nature on the Deep,
From all the cheats of Law he lives secure,
Nor does th'affronts of Palaces endure;
Sometimes the beaut'ous Marriageable Vine
He to the lusty Bridegroom Elm does joyn;
Sometimes he lops the barren Trees around,
And grafts new life into the fruitful wound;
Sometimes he sheers his Flock, and sometimes he
Stores up the golden Treasures of the Bee.
He sees the lowing Herds walk o'r the Plain,
Whilst neighb'ring Hills low back to them again:
And when the Season Rich as well as Gay,
All her Autumnal Bounty does display.
How is he pleas'd th' encreasing Use to see,
Of his well trusted Labors bend the tree.
Of which large shares, on the glad sacred daies
He gives to Friends, and to the Gods repays.
With how much joy do's he beneath some shade
By aged trees rev'rend embraces made,
His careless head on the fresh Green recline,
His head uncharg'd with Fear or with Design.
By him a River constantly complains,
The Birds above rejoyce with various strains,
And in the solemn Scene their *Orgies* keep
Like Dreams mixt with the Gravity of sleep,
Sleep which does alwayes there for entrance wait
And nought within against it shuts the gate.
    Nor does the roughest season of the sky,

Or sullen *Jove* all sports to him deny,
He runs the Mazes of the nimble Hare,
His well-mouth'd Dogs glad concert rends the air,
Or with game bolder, and rewarded more,
He drives into a Toil the foaming Bore,
Here flies the Hawk t'assault, and there the Net
To intercept the trav'lling Soul is set.
And all his malice, all his craft is shown
In innocent wars, on beasts and birds alone.
This is the life from all misfortunes free,
From thee the Great one, Tyrant Love, from Thee;
And if a chast and clean, though homely wife
Be added to the blessings of this Life,
Such as the antient Sun-burnt *Sabins* were,
Such as *Apulia*, frugal still, does bear,
Who makes her Children and the house her care.
And joyfully the work of Life does share,
Nor thinks her self too noble or too fine
To pin the Sheepfold or to milk the Kine,
Who waits at door against her Husband come
From rural duties, late, and wearied home,
Where she receives him with a kind embrace,
A chearful Fire, and a more chearful Face:
And fills the Bowl up to her homely Lord,
And with domestique plenty loads the Board.
Not all the lustful shel-fish of the Sea,
Drest by the wanton hand of Luxurie,
Nor *Ortalans*, nor *Godwits*, nor the rest
Of costly names that glorify a Feast,
Are at the Princely tables better cheer,
Then Lamb and Kid, Lettice and Olives here.

RICHARD CRASHAW

Out of Catullus

Come and let us live my Deare,
Let us love and never feare,
What the sowrest Fathers say:
Brightest *Sol* that dies to day
Lives againe as blith to morrow,
But if we darke sons of sorrow
Set; o then, how long a Night
Shuts the Eyes of our short light!
Then let amorous kisses dwell
On our lips, begin and tell
A Thousand, and a Hundred, score
An Hundred, and a Thousand more,
Till another Thousand smother
That, and that wipe of another.
Thus at last when we have numbred
Many a Thousand, many a Hundred;
Wee'l confound the reckoning quite,
And lose our selves in wild delight:
While our joyes so multiply,
As shall mocke the envious eye.

Upon the Death of a Gentleman

Faithlesse and fond Mortality,
Who will ever credit thee?
Fond and faithlesse thing! that thus,
In our best hopes beguilest us.
What a reckoning hast thou made,
Of the hopes in him we laid?

For life by volumes lengthened,
A Line or two, to speake him dead.
For the Laurell in his verse,
The sullen Cypresse o're his Herse.
For a silver-crowned Head,
A durty pillow in Death's Bed.
For so deare, so deep a trust,
Sad requitall, thus much dust!
Now though the blow that snatcht him hence,
Stopt the Mouth of Eloquence,
Though shee be dumbe e're since his Death,
Not us'd to speake but in his Breath,
Yet if at least shee not denyes,
The sad language of our eyes,
Wee are contented: for then this
Language none more fluent is.
Nothing speakes our Griefe so well
As to speake Nothing, Come then tell
Thy mind in Teares who e're Thou be,
That ow'st a Name to misery.
Eyes are vocall, Teares have Tongues,
And there be words not made with lungs;
Sententious showers, o let them fall,
Their cadence is Rhetoricall,.
Here's a Theame will drinke th'expence,
Of all thy watry Eloquence,
Weepe then, onely be exprest
Thus much, *Hee's Dead*, and weepe the rest.

JOHN, LORD CUTTS

The Innocent Gazer

Lovely Lucinda, blame not me,
   If on your beauteous looks I gaze;
How can I help it, when I see
   Something so charming in your face?

That like a bright, unclouded sky,
   When in the air the sun-beams play,
It ravishes my wond'ring eye,
   And warms me with a pleasing ray.

An air so settled, so serene,
   And yet so gay, and easy too,
On all our plains I have not seen
   In any other nymph but you.

But fate forbids me to design
   The mighty conquest of your breast;
And I had rather torture mine,
   Than rob you of one minute's rest.

JOHN DANCER

The Variety

Thou sai'st I swore I lov'd thee best,
    And that my heart liv'd in thy breast;
    And now thou wondrest much that I
Should what I swore then, much deny,
And upon this thou taxest me
With faithlessnesse, inconstancy:
    Thou hast no reason so to do,
    Who can't dissemble ne'r must wooe.

That so I lov'd thee 'tis confest,
But 'twas because I judg'd thee best,
For then I thought that thou alone
Wast vertue's, beautie's paragon:
But now that the deceit I find,
To love thee still were to be blind;
    And I must needs confess to thee
    I love in love variety.

Alas! should I love thee alone,
In a short time I should love none;
Who on one well-lov'd feeds, yet,
Once being cloy'd, of all, loaths it;
Would'st thou be subject to a fate
To make me change my love to hate?
    Blame me not then, since 'tis for love
    Of thee, that I inconstant prove.

And yet in truth 'tis constancy,
For which I am accus'd by thee;
To nature those inconstant are,
Who fix their love on one that's faire;

Why did she, but for our delight,
Present such numbers to our sight?
   'Mongst all the earthly kings, there's none
   Contented with one Crown alone.

GEORGE DANIEL

Pure Platonicke

Not Roses, joyn'd with Lillies, make
Her Faire, nor though her Eyes be blacke
And glorious, as th' Etheriall Queene,
Are they my wonder; I have seene
Beautie, and scorn'd it, at fowerteene.

Not to have a Skin, as smooth
As Christall; nor a Lip, nor mouth,
Bright Citherea's ornament,
Move me at all; let them invent
A Dresse, to move new blandishment,

I am not taken; not the Faire
Enchantments, of well-order'd haire,
Not a Leg, nor Foot, nor hand,
Nor the parts wee understand
Most attractive, mee command.

Though I give all Beautie prise
To the value of my Eyes;
Yet I doe not love a Face,
Nor dote upon the outward grace;
These respects, can have noe place.

Wee distinguish nothing to
The outward Forme, as Lovers doe;
Nor value by the rule, of Sence.
Wee know noe Sexes difference,
Equall in Pre'eminence

To the Sympathising mind,
Neither hinder, neither bind;

But in either's brest wee move,
And Affections Equall prove:
This is pure Platonicke Love.

Anti-Platonicke

Noe longer torture mee, in dreams
Of reservations, and Extream's;
Nature, never yet, in Two
Such a Calmenes, did bestow,
As you would pretend unto.

Give me buxome Youth; and Blood,
Quicknd, in the understood
Caution of Love; a free desire
To meet with mine, in Equall Fire,
And doe the Act, wee both Conspire.

In the free, and Common way,
I would all my heats allay.
I have little Skill in love;
Little leasure, to Emprove
But by Natures precepts move.

In everie Step, I tread that path,
And to new Dictates, want a Faith;
If I see her yonge, and Faire,
Fresh, and Blith, and fitt to payre;
I have whol'some wishes nere.

My blood burnes; I cannot hold;
Strong desires make us bold;
I must utter all I thinke,
Not in a Question, or a winke:
Such mustie follies, ever stinke.

But I urge, and presse it close;
All I know, or you suppose;
Women are noe longer Chast
Then untempted; they would tast
Men, with Equall Heat, and Hast.

SIR WILLIAM DAVENANT

Song
The Souldier going to the Field

Preserve thy sighs, unthrifty girle!
    To purifie the ayre;
Thy tears to thrid, instead of pearle,
    On bracelets of thy hair.

The trumpet makes the eccho hoarse,
    And wakes the louder drum;
Expenc of grief gains no remorse,
    When sorrow should be dumb.

For I must go where lazy Peace
    Will hide her drouzy head;
And, for the sport of kings, encrease
    The number of the dead.

But first I'le chide thy cruel theft:
    Can I in war delight,
Who being of my heart bereft,
    Can have no heart to fight?

Thou know'st the sacred laws of old
    Ordain'd a thief should pay,
To quit him of his theft, seavenfold
    What he had stoln away.

Thy payment shall but double be;
    O then with speed resign
My own seduced heart to me,
    Accompani'd with thine.

CHARLES SACKVILLE
EARL OF DORSET

(Phillis for Shame let us Improve)

Phillis for shame let us improve
    A thousand sev'ral wayes,
These few short Minutes snatchd by Love
    From many tedious days.

Whilst you want courage to despise
    The Censures of the Grave;
For all the tyrants in your eyes,
    Your heart is but a slave.

My Love is full of noble pride,
    And never shall submit,
To let that Fop discretion ride
    In triumph over wit.

False friends I have as well as you,
    Who daily counsel me,
Fame and ambition to pursue,
    And leave off loving thee.

When I the least belief bestow
    On what such fools advise:
May I be dull enough to grow
    Most miserable wise.

Song

Dorinda's sparkling wit, and eyes,
    United, cast too fierce a light,

Which blazes high, but quickly dies,
 Pains not the heart, but hurts the sight.

Love is a calmer, gentler joy,
 Smooth are his looks, and soft his pace;
Her Cupid is a black-guard boy,
 That runs his link full in your face.

On the Countess of Dorchester Mistress to King James II. 1680

I

Tell me, Dorinda, why so gay,
 Why such Embroid'ry, Fringe, and Lace?
Can any Dresses find a Way,
To stop th' Approaches of Decay,
 And mend a ruin'd Face?

II

Wilt Thou still sparkle in the Box,
 Still ogle in the Ring?
Canst Thou forget thy Age and Pox?
Can all that shines on Shells and Rocks
 Make thee a fine young Thing?

III

So have I seen in Larder dark
 Of Veal and lucid Loin;
Replete with many a brilliant Spark,
(As wise Philosophers remark)
 At once both stink and shine.

Song

I

Methinks the poor town has been troubled too long,
With Phyllis and Chloris in every song,
But fools, who at once had both love and despair,
And will never leave calling them cruel and fair;
Which justly provokes me in rhyme to express
The truth that I know of bonny Black Bess.

II

This Bess of my heart, this Bess of my soul,
Has a skin white as milk, and hair as black as a coal;
She's plump, yet with ease you may span round her waist,
But her round swelling thighs can scarce be embrac'd;
Her belly is soft, not a word of the rest:
But I know what I think, when I drink to the best.

III

The plowman and 'squire, the arranter clown,
At home she subdued in her poragon gown;
But now she adorns both the boxes and pit,
And the proudest town gallants are forc'd to submit;
All hearts fall a leaping wherever she comes,
And beat day and night, like my Lord Craven's drums.

IV

I dare not permit her to come to Whitehall,
For she'd outshine the ladies, paint, jewels, and all:
If a lord should but whisper his love in the crowd,
She'd sell him a bargain, and laugh out aloud:
Then the Queen, overhearing what Betty did say,
Would send Mr. Roper to take her away.

V

But to those that have had my dear Bess in their arms,
She's gentle, and knows how to soften her charms;
And to every beauty can add a new grace,
Having learn'd how to lisp, and to trip in her pace;
And with head on one side, and a languishing eye,
To kill us by looking as if she would die.

Song

*Written at Sea, in the first Dutch War, 1665,
the Night before the Engagement*

I

To all you Ladies now at Land
    We Men at Sea indite;
But first wou'd have you understand
    How hard it is to write;
The Muses now, and Neptune too,
We must implore to write to you.
    With a fa, la, la, la, la.

II

For tho' the Muses should prove kind,
    And fill our empty Brain;
Yet if rough Neptune rouse the Wind,
    To wave the Azure Main,
Our Paper, Pen, and Ink, and we,
Roll up and down our Ships at Sea.
    With a fa, etc.

III

Then, if we write not by each Post,
　　Think not we are unkind;
Nor yet conclude our Ships are lost
　　By Dutchmen, or by Wind:
Our Tears we'll send a speedier Way,
The Tide shall bring 'em twice a day.
　　With a fa, etc.

IV

The King, with Wonder and Surprise,
　　Will swear the Seas grow bold;
Because the Tides will higher rise,
　　Than e'er they us'd of old:
But let him know it is our Tears
Bring Floods of Grief to Whitehall Stairs.
　　With a fa, etc.

V

Should foggy Opdam chance to know
　　Our sad and dismal Story;
The Dutch would scorn so weak a Foe,
　　And quit their Fort at Goeree:
For what Resistance can they fine
From Men who've left their Hearts behind?
　　With a fa, etc.

VI

Let Wind and Weather do its worst,
Be You to Us but kind;
Let Dutchmen vapour, Spaniards curse,
　　No Sorrow we shall find:

'Tis then no Matter how Things go,
Or who's our Friend, or who's our Foe,
    With a fa, etc.

VII

To pass our tedious Hours away,
    We throw a merry Main;
Or else at serious ombre play;
    But, why should we in vain
Each other's Ruin thus pursue?
We were undone when we left you.
    With a fa, etc.

VIII

But now our Fears tempestuous grow,
    And cast our Hopes away;
Whilst you, regardless of our Woe,
    Sit careless at a Play:
Perhaps permit some happier Man
To Kiss you Hand, or flirt your Fan.
    With a fa, etc.

IX

When any mournful Tune you hear,
    That dies in every Note;
As if it sigh'd with each Man's Care,
    For being so remote:
Think how often Love we've made
To you, when all those Tunes were play'd.
    With a fa, etc.

X

In Justice you cannot refuse,
    To think of our Distress;

When we for Hopes of Honour lose
    Our certain Happiness;
All those Designs are but to prove
Ourselves more worthy of your Love.
    With a fa, etc.

XI

And now we've told you all our Loves,
    And likewise all our fears;
In Hopes this Declaration moves
    Some Pity for our Tears:
Let's hear of no Inconstancy,
We have too much of that at Sea.
    With a fa, la, la, la, la.

JOHN DRYDEN

A Song: from *The Spanish Fryar*

I

Farewell ungratefull Traytor,
   Farewell my perjur'd Swain
Let never injur'd Creature
   Believe a Man again.
The Pleasure of Possessing
Surpasses all Expressing,
But 'tis too short a Blessing,
   And Love too long a Pain.

II

'Tis easie to deceive us
   In pity of our Pain,
But when we love you leave us
   To rail at you in vain.
Before we have descry'd it
There is no Bliss beside it;
But she that once has try'd it
   Will never love again.

III

The Passion you pretended
   Was onely to obtain,
But when the Charm is ended
   The Charmer you disdain.
Your Love by ours we measure
Till we have lost our Treasure,
But Dying is a Pleasure,
   When Living is a Pain.

Rondelay

Chloe found Amyntas lying
  All in Tears, upon the Plain;
Sighing to himself, and crying,
  Wretched I, to love in vain!
Kiss me, Dear, before my dying;
  Kiss me once, and ease my pain!

Sighing to himself, and crying
  Wretched I, to love in vain:
Ever scorning and denying
  To reward your faithful Swain:
Kiss me, Dear, before my dying;
  Kiss me once, and ease my pain!

Ever scorning, and denying
  To reward your faithful Swain.
Chloe, laughing at his crying,
  Told him that he lov'd in vain:
Kiss me, Dear, before my dying;
  Kiss me once, and ease my pain!

Chloe, laughing at his crying,
  Told him that he lov'd in vain:
But repenting, and complying,
  When he kiss'd, she kiss'd again:
Kiss'd him up, before his dying;
  Kiss'd him up, and eas'd his pain.

A Song: from Amphitrion

Celia, that I once was blest
  Is now the Torment of my Brest;

Since to curse me, you bereave me
Of the Pleasures I possest:
Cruel Creature, to deceive me!
  First to love, and then to leave me!

Had you the Bliss refus'd to grant,
  Then I have never known the want:
  But possessing once the Blessing,
  Is the Cause of my Complaint:
Once possessing is but tasting;
  'Tis no Bliss that is not lasting.

  Celia now is mine no more;
  But I am hers; and must adore:
  Nor to leave her will endeavour;
  Charms, that captiv'd me before,
  No unkindness can dissever;
  Love that's true, is Love for ever.

A Song: from *Sylvoe*

I

Go tell *Amynta* gentle Swain,
I wou'd not die nor dare complain,
Thy tuneful Voice with numbers joyn,
Thy words will more prevail than mine;
To Souls oppress'd and dumb with grief.
The Gods ordain this kind releif;
That Musick shou'd in sounds convey,
What dying Lovers dare not say.

II

A Sigh or Tear perhaps she'll give,
But love on pitty cannot live.

Tell her that Hearts for Hearts were made,
And love with love is only paid.
Tell her my pains so fast encrease,
That soon they will be past redress;
But ah! the Wretch that speechless lyes,
Attends but Death to close his Eyes.

A Song: from *Tyrannick Love*

Ah how sweet it is to love,
Ah how gay is young desire!
And what pleasing pains we prove
When we first approach Loves fire!
   Pains of Love be sweeter far
   Than all other pleasures are.

Sighs which are from Lovers blown,
Do but gently heave the Heart;
Ev'n the tears they shed alone
Cure, like trickling Balm their smart.
   Lovers when they love their breath,
   Bleed away in easie death.

Love and Time with reverence use,
Treat 'em like a parting friend:
Nor the golden gifts refuse
Which in youth sincere they send:
   For each year their price is more,
   And they less simple than before.

Love, like Spring-tides full and high,
Swells in every youthful vein:
But each Tide does less supply,
Till they quite shrink in again:
   If a flow in Age appear,
   'Tis but rain, and runs not clear.

A Song: from *An Evening's Love*

Damon	Celimena, of my heart,
	None shall e'er bereave you:
	If, with your good leave, I may
	Quarrel with you once a day,
	I will never leave you.
Celimena	Passion's but an empty name
	Where respect is wanting:
	Damon you mistake your ayme;
	Hang your heart, and burn your flame,
	If you must be ranting.
Damon	Love as dull and muddy is,
	As decaying liquor:
	Anger sets it on the lees,
	And refines it by degrees,
	Till workes it quicker.
Celimena	Love by quarrels to beget
	Wisely you endeavour;
	With a grave Physician's wit
	Who to cure an Ague fit
	Put me in a Feavor.
Damon	Anger rouzes love to fight,
	And his only bayt is,
	'Tis the spurre to dull delight,
	And is but an eager bite,
	When desire at height is.
Celimena	If such drops of heat can fall
	In our wooing weather;
	If such drops of heat can fall,
	We shall have the Devil and all
	When we come together.

A Song: from *An Evening's Love*

Calm was the Even, and cleer was the Skie
   And the new budding flowers did spring,
When all alone went *Amyntas* and I
   To hear the sweet Nightingale sing;
I sate, and he laid him down by me;
   But scarcely his breath he could draw;
For when with a fear he began to draw near,
   He was dash'd with A ha ha ha ha!

He blush'd to himself, and lay still for a while,
   And his modesty curb'd his desire;
But streight I convinc'd all his fear with a smile,
   Which added new flames to his fire.
O Sylvia, said he, you are cruel,
   To keep your poor Lover in awe;
Then once more he prest with his hands to my brest,
   But was dash'd with A ha ha ha ha.

I knew 'twas his passion that caus'd all his fear;
   And therefore I pity's his case:
I whisper'd him softly there's no body near,
   And layd my cheek close to his face:
But as he grew bolder and bolder,
   A Shepherd came by us and saw;
And just as our bliss we began with a kiss,
   He laughed out with A ha ha ha ha.

A Song: from *An Evening's Love*

You charm'd me not with that fair face
   Though it was all divine:

To be anothers is the Grace,
　　That makes me wish you mine.
The Gods and Fortune take their part
　　Who like young Monarchs fight;
And boldly dare invade that heart
　　Which is anothers right.
First mad with hope we undertake
　　To pull up every barr;
But once possess'd, we faintly make
　　A dull defensive warr,
Now every friend is turn'd a foe
　　In hope to get our store:
And passion makes us Cowards grow,
　　Which made us brave before.

A Song: from *Marriage-a-la-Mode*

Whil'st *Alexis* lay prest
In her Arms, he lov'd best,
With his hands round her neck,
And his head on her breast,
He found the fierce pleasure too hasty to stay,
And his soul in the tempest just flying away.

When *Cælia* saw this,
With a sigh, and a kiss,
She cry'd, Oh my dear, I am robb'd of my bliss;
'Tis unkind to your Love, and unfaithfully done,
To leave me behind you, and die all alone.

The Youth, though in haste,
And breathing his last,
In pity dy'd slowly, while she dy'd more fast;
Till at length she cry'd, Now, my dear, now let us go,
Now die, my *Alexis*, and I will die too.

Thus intranc'd they did lie,
Till *Alexis* did try
To recover new breath, that again he might die:
Then often they di'd; but the more they did so,
The Nymph di'd more quick, and the Shepherd more slow.

Horace, Lib. I. Ode 9

I

Behold yon Mountains hoary height
    Made higher with new Mounts of Snow;
Again behold the Winters weight
    Oppress the lab'ring Woods below:
And streams with Icy fetters bound,
Benum'd and cramt to solid ground.

II

With well heap'd Logs dissolve the cold
    And feed the genial hearth with fires;
Produce the Wine, that makes us bold,
    And sprightly Wit and Love inspires:
For what hereafter shall betide,
God, if 'tis worth his care, provide.

III

Let him alone with what he made,
    To toss and turn the World below;
At his command the storms invade;
    The winds by his Commission blow;
Till with a Nod he bids 'em cease,
And then the Calm returns, and all is peace.

I

IV

To morrow and her works defie,
   Lay hold upon the present hour,
And snatch the pleasures passing by,
   To put them out of Fortunes pow'r:
Nor love, nor love's delights disdain,
What e're you get'st to day is gain.

V

Secure those golden early joyes,
   That Youth unsowr'd with sorrow bears,
E're with'ring time the taste destroyes,
   With sickness and unweildy years!
For active sports, for pleasing rest,
This is the time to be possesst;
The best is but in season best.

VI

The pointed hour of promis'd bliss,
   The pleasing whisper in the dark,
The half unwilling willing kiss,
   The laugh that guides thee to the mark,
When the kind Nymph wou'd coyness feign,
And hides but to be found again,
These, these are joyes the Gods for Youth ordain.

THOMAS DUFFETT

To Francelia

In cruelty you greater are,
  Then those fierce Tyrants who decreed,
The Noblest prisoner ta'n in war,
  Should to their gods a Victim bleed.

A year of pleasures and delight,
  The happy prisoner there obtain'd,
And three whole daies e'r death's long night,
  In pow'r unlimited he reign'd.

To your Victorious Eyes I gave
  My heart a willing Sacrifice;
A tedious year have been your slave;
  Felt all the pains Hate could devise.

But two short hours of troubl'd Bliss,
  For all my suffrings you restore;
And wretched I must die for this,
  And never never meet you more.

Never, how dismally it sounds!
  If l must feel eternal pain,
Close up a while my bleeding wounds,
  And let me have my three daies' reign.

THOMAS D'URFEY

A Song

Boast no more fond Love, thy Power,
Mingling Passions sweet and sower;
Bow to *Caelia*, show thy Duty,
Caelia sways the World of Beauty:
Venus now must kneel before her,
And admiring Crowds adore her.

Like the Sun that gilds the Morning,
Caelia shines, but more adorning;
She like Fate, can wound a Lover,
Goddess like too, can recover:
She can Kill, or save from dying,
The Transported Soul is flying.

Sweeter than the blooming Rose is,
Whiter than the falling Snow is;
Then such Eyes the Great Creator
Chose as Lamps to kindle Nature;
Curst is he that can refuse her,
Ah, hard Fate, that I must loose her.

To Cynthia.   A Song

Born with the Vices of my kind,
   I were Inconstant too;
Dear *Cynthia*, could I rambling find
   More Beauty than in you.

The rowling Surges of my Blood,
   By Virtue now ebb'd low;

Should a new Shower encrease the Flood,
    Too soon would overflow.

But Frailty when thy Face I see,
    Does modestly retire;
Uncommon must her Graces be,
    Whose look can bound desire.

Not to my Virtue, but thy Power,
    This Constancy is due;
When change it self can give no more,
    'Tis easie to be true.

A Song

The Night her blackest Sables wore,
    And gloomy were the Skies;
And glitt'ring Stars there were no more,
    Than those in *Stella's* Eyes:
When at her Father's Gate I knock'd,
    Where I had often been,
And Shrowded only with her Smock,
    The fair one let me in.

Fast lock'd within my close Embrace,
    She trembling lay asham'd;
Her swelling Breast, and glowing Face,
    And every touch inflam'd:
My eager Passion I obey'd,
    Resolv'd the Fort to win;
And her fond Heart was soon betray'd,
    To yield and let me in.

Then! then! beyond expressing,
    Immortal was the Joy;

I knew no greater blessing,
   So great a God was I:
And she transported with delight,
   Oft pray'd me come again;
And kindly vow'd that every Night,
   She'd rise and let me in.

But, oh! at last she prov'd with Bern,
   And sighing sat and dull;
And I that was a much concern'd,
   Look'd then just like a Fool:
Her lovely Eyes with tears run o'er,
   Repenting her rash Sin;
She sigh'd and curs'd the fatal hour,
   That e'er She let me in.

But who could cruelly deceive,
   Or from such Beauty part;
I lov'd her so, I could not leave
   The Charmer of my Heart:
But Wedded and conceal'd the Crime,
   Thus all was well again;
And now she thanks the blessed Time,
   That e'er she let me in.

Brother Solon's Hunting Song.
Sung by Mr Doggett

Tantivee, tivee, tivee, tivee, High and Low,
Hark, hark how the Merry, merry Horn does blow,
As through the Lanes and Meadows we go.
   As Puss has run over the Down;
When Ringwood and Rockwood, and Jowler & Spring,

And Thunder and Wonder made all the Woods ring,
And Horsemen and Footmen, hey ding, a ding ding,
   Who envies the Pleasure and State of a Crown.

Then follow, follow, follow, follow Jolly boys,
Keep in with the Beagles now whilst the Scent lies,
The fiery Fac'd God is just ready to rise,
   Whose Beams all our Pleasure controuls;
Whils over the Mountains and Valleys we rowl,
And *Wat's* fatal Knell in each hollow we toll;
And in the next Cottage tope off a full Bowl,
   What Pleasure like Hunting can cherish the Soul.

The Winchester Wedding; or Ralph of Redding, and Black Bess of the Green

At *Winchester* was a Wedding,
   The like was never seen,
Twixt lusty *Ralph* of *Redding*,
   And bonny black *Bess* of the *Green*:
The Fidlers were Crouding before,
   Each Lass was as fine as a Queen;
There was a Hundred and more,
   For all the Country came in:
Brisk *Robin* led *Rose* so fair,
   She look'd like a Lilly o' th' Vale;
And Ruddy Fac'd *Harry* led *Mary*
   And *Roger* led bouncing *Nell*.

With *Tommy* came smiling *Katy*,
   He help'd her over the Stile;
And swore there was none so pretty,
   In forty, and forty long Mile:
Kit gave a Green-Gown to *Betty*,

And lent her his Hand to rise;
But *Jenny* was jeer'd by *Watty*,
   For looking blue under the Eyes:
Thus merrily Chatting all,
   They pass'd to the *Bride-house* along;
With *Johnny* and pretty fac'd *Nanny*,
   The fairest of all the throng.

The Bride came out to meet 'em,
   Afraid the Dinner was spoil'd;
And usher'd 'em in to treat 'em,
   With *Bak'd*, and *Roasted*, and *Boil'd:*
The Lads were so frolick and jolly,
   For each had his Love by his side;
But *Willy* was Melancholly,
   For he had a Mind to the Bride:
Then *Philip* begins her Health,
   And turns a Beer Glass on his Thumb;
But *Jenkin* was reckon'd for Drinking,
   The best in *Christendom*.

And now they had Din'd, advancing
   Into the midst of the *Hall*;
The Fidlers struck up for Dancing,
   And *Jeremy* led up the *Brawl:*
But *Margery* kept a quarter,
   A Lass that was proud of her Pelf,
Cause *Arthur* had stolen her Garter,
   And swore he would tie it himself:
She struggl'd, and blush'd, and frown'd,
   And ready with Anger to cry;
'Cause *Arthur* with tying her Garter,
   Had slip'd his Hand too high.

And now for throwing the Stocking,
   The Bride away was led;

The Bridegroom got Drunk and was knocking,
    For Candles to light 'em to Bed:
But *Robin* that found him Silly,
    Most friendly took him aside;
The while that his *Wife* with *Willy*,
    Was playing at *Hoopers-hide:*
And now the warm *Game* begins,
    The *Critical Minute* was come;
And chatting, and Billing, and Kissing,
    Went merrily round the Room.

Pert *Stephen* was kind to *Betty*,
    And blith as a Bird in the Spring;
And *Tommy* was so to *Katy*,
    And Wedded her with a *Rush Ring:*
Sukey that Danc'd with the *Cushion*,
    An Hour from the Room had been gone;
And *Barnaby* knew by her Blushing,
    That some other Dance had been done:
And thus of Fifty fair Maids,
    That came to the Wedding with Men;
Scarce Five of the Fifty was left ye,
    That so did return again.

'EPHELIA'

Song

Know, Celadon, in vain you use
   These little Arts to me:
Though Strephon did my Heart refuse
   I cannot give it thee;
His harsh Refusal hath not brought
   Its Value yet so low,
That what was worth that Shepherd's Thoughts
   I shou'd on You bestow.

Nor can I love my Strephon less
   For his ungrateful Pride,
Though Honour does, I must confess
   My guilty Passion chide:
That lovely Youth I still adore,
   Though now it be in vain;
But yet of him I ask no more
   Than Pity for my Pain.

Song

You wrong me, Strephon, when you say
   I'me Jealous or Severe,
Did I not see you Kiss and Play
   With all you came a-neer?
Say, did I ever Chide for this,
   Or cast one Jealous Eye
On the bold Nymphs that snatch'd my Bliss
   While I stood wishing by?

Yet though I never disapprov'd
   This modish Liberty,
I thought in them you only lov'd
   Change and Variety:
I vainly thought my Charms so strong,
   And you so much my Slave,
No Nymph had Pow'r to do me Wrong,
   Or break the Chains I gave.

But when you seriously Address
   With all your winning Charms
Unto a Servile Shepherdess,
   I'le throw you from my Arms:
I'de rather chuse you should make Love
   To every Face you see,
Than Mopsa's dull Admirer prove
   And let Her Rival me.

SIR GEORGE ETHEREGE

Song

If she be not as kind as fair,
  But peevish and unhandy,
Leave her—she's only worth the care
  Of some spruce Jack-a-dandy.

I would not have thee such an ass,
  Hadst thou ne'er so much leisure,
To sigh and whine for such a lass
  Whose pride's above her pleasure.

Make much of every buxom girl
  Which needs but little courting;
Her value is above the pearl,
  That takes delight in sporting.

Silvia

The nymph that undoes me is fair and unkind,
No less than a wonder by Nature designed;
She's the grief of my heart, the joy of my eye,
And the cause of a flame that never can die.

Her mouth, from whence wit still obligingly flows,
Has the beautiful blush and the smell of the rose;
Love and destiny both attend on her will,
She wounds with a look, with a frown she can kill.

The desperate lover can hope no redress
Where beauty and rigor are both in excess;

In Silvia they meet, so unhappy am I,
Who sees her must love and who loves her must die.

Song

Tell me no more I am deceived;
   While Silvia seems so kind,
And takes such care to be believed,
   The cheat I fear to find.
To flatter me, should falsehood lie
   Concealed in her soft youth,
A thousand times I'd rather die
   Than see the unhappy truth.

My love all malice shall outbrave,
   Let fops in libels rail;
If she the appearances will save,
   No scandal can prevail.
She makes me think I have her heart,
   How much for that is due?
Though she but act the tender part,
   The joy she gives is true.

The Rival

Of all the torments, all the cares
   With which our lives are cursed,
Of all the plagues a lover bears,
   Sure rivals are the worst.

By partners in another kind
   Afflictions easier grow,

In love alone we hate to find
　Companions in our woe.

Cynthia, for all the pains you see
　Are laboring in my breast,
I beg not that you'd pity me
　But that you'd slight the rest.

How great so e'er your rigors are,
　With them alone I'll cope;
I can endure my own despair
　But not another's hope.

A Letter to Lord Middleton

From hunting whores and haunting play,
And minding nothing else all day
(And all the night too you will say),
To make grave legs in formal fetters,
Converse with fops, and write dull letters;
To go to bed 'twixt eight and nine,
And sleep away my precious time
In such an idle sneaking place,
Where vice and folly hide their face,
And, in a troublesome disguise,
The wife seems modest, husband wise.
For pleasure here has the same fate
Which does attend Affairs of State:
The plague of ceremony infects,
Even in love, the softer sex,
Who an essential will neglect
Rather than lose the least respect;
With regular approach we storm,
And never visit but in form—

That is, sending to know before
At what o'clock they'll play the whore.
The nymphs are constant, gallants private,
One scarce can guess who 'tis they drive at;
This seems to me a scurvy fashion,
Who have been bred in a free nation,
With liberty of speech and passion.
Yet I cannot forbear to spark it
And make the best of a bad market;
Meeting with one by chance kind-hearted,
Who no preliminaries started,
I entered beyond expectation
Into a close negotiation
Of which hereafter a relation.
Humble to fortune, not her slave,
I still was pleased with what she gave,
And with a firm and cheerful mind
I steer my course with every wind
To all the ports she has designed.

MILDMAY FANE
EARL OF WESTMORELAND

My Happy Life
To a Friend

Dearest in Friendship, if you'll know
Where I my self, and how, bestow,
Especially when as I range,
Guided by Nature, to love change,
Beleeve, it is not to advance
Or add to my inheritance;
Seeking t'engross by Power amiss
What any other Man calls his:
But full contented with my owne,
I let all other things alone;
Which better t'enjoy without strife,
I settle to a Countrey life.
And in a sweet retirement there
Cherish all Hopes, but banish fear,
Offending none; so for defence
Arm'd Capapee with Innocence,
I do dispose of my time thus,
To make it more propitious.
   First, my God serv'd, I doe commend
The rest to some choice Book or Friend,
Wherein I may such Treasure finde
T'inrich my nobler part, the Minde.
And that my Body Health comprise,
Use too some moderate Exercise;
Whether invited to the field
To see what Pastime that can yield,
With horse, or hound, or hawk, or t'bee
More taken with a well-grown Tree;
Under whose Shades I may reherse

The holy Layes of Sacred Verse;
Whilst in the Branches pearched higher,
The wind'd Crew sit as in a quier:
This seems to me a better noise
Than Organs, or the dear-bought voice
From Pleaders breath in Court and Hall
At any time is stockt withall:
For here one may, (if marking well),
Observe the Plaintive Philomel
Bemoan her sorrows, and the Thrush
Plead safety through Defendant Bush;
The Popingay in various die
Performes the Sergeant, and the Pie
Chatters, as if she would revive
The Old Levite prerogative,
And bring new Rotchets in again;
Till Crowes and Jackdaws in disdain
Of her Pide-feathers chase her thence,
To yeeld to their preheminence.
For you must know't observ'd of late,
That Reformation in the State
Begets no less by imitation
Amidst this chirping feather'd Nation;
Cuckoes Ingrate and Woodcocks some
Here are, which cause they't seasons come,
May be compar'd to such as stand
At Terms, and their returns command.
And, lest Authority take cold,
Here's th'Ivye's guest of wonder, th'Owl,
Rufft like a Judge, and with a Beak,
As it would give the charge and speak:
Then 'tis the Goose and Buzzards art
Alone, t'perform the Clients part;
For neither Dove nor Pigeon shall,
Whilst they are both exempt from gall.
The Augur Hern, and soaring Kite,

Kalendar weather in their flight,
As doe the Cleanlier Ducks, when they
Dive voluntary, wash, prune, play,
With the fair Cygnet, whose delight
Is to out-vie the snow in white.
And therefore alwayes seeks to hide
Her feet, lest they allay her pride.
The Moor-hen, Dobchick, Water-rail,
With little Washdish or Wagtail;
The Finch, the Sparrow, Jenny Wren,
With Robin that's so kinde to men;
The Whitetail and Tom Tit obey
Their seasons, bill and tread, then lay;
The Lyrick Lark doth early rise,
And, mounting, payes her sacrifice;
Whilst from some hedge, or close of furrs,
The Partridge calls its Mate, and churrs;
And that the Countrey seem more pleasant,
Each heath hath Powt, and wood yeelds Phesant;
Junoe's delight, with Cock and Hens,
Turkies, are my Domestick friends;
Nor doe I bird of Prey inlist,
But what I carry on my Fist;
Now not to want a Court, a King-
Fisher is here with Purple wing,
Who brings me to the spring-head, where
Crystall is Lymbeckt all the yeere,
And every Drop distil'd, implies
An Ocean of Felicities;
Whilst calculating, it spins on,
And turns the Pebbles one by one,
Administering to eye and eare
New Stars, and musick like the Sphere;
When every Purle Calcin'd doth run,
And represent such from the Sun.
   Devouring Pike here hath no place,

Nor is it stor'd with Roach or Dace;
The Chub or Cheven not appeare,
Nor Miller's Thumbs, nor Gudgeons here,
But nobler Trowts, beset with stones
Of Rubie and of Diamonds,
Bear greatest sway; yet some intrench,
As sharp-finn'd Pearch, and healing Tench;
The stream's too pure for Carp to lie,
Subject to perspicuitie;
For it must here be understood
There are no beds of sand and Mud,
But such a Gravell as might pose
The best of Scholars to disclose,
And books and learning all confute,
Being clad in water Tissue sute.
These cool delights help'd with the air
Fann'd from the Branches of the fair
Old Beech, or Oak, enchantments tie
To every sense's facultie;
And master all those powers should give
The will any prerogative:
Yet when the Scorching Noon-dayes heat
Incommodates the Lowing Neat
Or Bleating flock, hither each one
Hasts to be my Companion.
And when the Western Skie with red
Roses bestrews the Day-star's bed,
The wholesome Maid comes out to Milk
In russet-coats, but skin like Silk;
Which, though the Sun and Air dies brown,
Will yeeld to none of all the Town
For softness, and her breath's sweet smell
Doth all the new-milcht Kie excell:
She knows no rotten teeth, nor hair
Bought, or Complexion t'make her fair,
But is her own fair wind and dress,

145

Not envying Citie's happiness:
Yet as she would extend some pitty
To the drain'd Neat, she frames a ditty
Which doth inchant the beast, untill
It patiently lets her Paile fill;
This doth the babbling Eccho catch
And so at length to me't doth reach.
Straight roused up, I verdict pass,
Concluding from this bonny Lass
And the Birds' strains, 'tis hard to say
Which taught Notes first, or she, or they.
Thus ravish'd, as the night draws on
Its sable Curtain, in I'm gon
To my poor Cell, which 'cause 'tis mine,
I judge it doth all else out-shine:
Hung with content and weather-proof,
Though neither Pavement nor roof
Borrow from Marble-quarr below,
Or from those Hills where Cedars grow.
There I embrace and kiss my Spouse,
Who, like the Vesta to the house,
A Sullibub prepares to show
By care and love what I must owe.
    Then calling in the Spawn and frie,
Who whilst they live ne'er let us die,
But every face is hers or mine,
Though minted yet in lesser Coin,
She takes an Apple, I a Plumbe,
Encouragements for all and some
Till in return they crown the herth
With innocent and harmless merth,
Which sends us Joyfull to our rest,
More than a thousand others blest.

SIR RICHARD FANSHAWE

A Rose

Blown in the morning, thou shalt fade ere noon:
    What boots a life which in such haste forsakes thee?
    Th'art wond'rous frolick being to die so soon:
    And passing proud a little colour makes thee.

If thee thy brittle beauty so deceives,
    Know then the thing that swells thee is thy bane;
    For the same beauty doth in bloody Leaves
    The sentence of thy early death contain.

Some clowns coarse lungs will poyson thy sweet flow'r
    If by the careless Plow thou shalt be torn:
    And many *Herods* lie in wait each hour
    To murther thee as soon as thou art born:

Nay, force thy bud to blow; their tyrant breath
Anticipating life, to hasten Death.

OWEN FELLTHAM

Contentment
Translation from Martial

Things that can bless a life, and please,
Sweetest Martial, they are these:
A store well left, not gain'd with toil,
A house thine own, and pleasant soyl;
No strife, small state, a mind at peace,
Free strength, and limbs free from disease;
Wise Innocence, friends like and good,
Unarted-meat, kind neighbourhood;
No drunken rest, from cares yet free,
No sadning spouse, yet chaste to thee;
Sleeps, that long nights abbreviate;
Because 'tis liking, thy wish't state;
Nor fear'd, nor joy'd, at death or fate.

The Sun and Wind

Why think'st thou, fool, thy Beautie's rayes
  Should flame my colder heart,
When thy disdain shall several wayes
  Such piercing blasts impart?

Seest not those beams that guild the day,
  (Though they be hot and fierce),
Yet have not heat nor power to stay,
  When winds their strength disperse.

So, though thy Sun heats my desire,
  Yet know thy coy disdain

Falls like a storm on that young fire,
So blowes me cool again.

This Ensuing Copy the Late Printer hath been pleased to Honour, by mistaking it among those of the Most Ingenious and Too Early Lost, Sir John Suckling

When, Dearest, I but think on thee,
   Methinks all things that lovely be
Are present, and my soul delighted:
For beauties that from worth arise,
Are like the grace of Deities,
   Still present with us, though unsighted.

Thus while I sit and sigh the day,
With all his spreading lights away,
   Till nights black wings do overtake me:
Thinking on thee, thy beauties then,
As sudden lights do sleeping men,
   So they by their bright rayes awake me.

Thus absence dies, and dying proves
No absence can consist with Loves,
   That do partake of fair perfection:
Since in the darkest night they may
By their quick motion find a way
   To see each other by reflection.

The waving Sea can with such flood,
Bath some high Palace that hath stood
   Far from the Main up in the River:
Oh think not then but love can do
As much, for that's an Ocean too,
   That flows not every day, but ever.

THOMAS FLATMAN

The Advice

Poor Celia once was very fair,
   A quick bewitching eye she had,
Most neatly looked her braided hair,
   Her dainty cheeks would make you mad,
Upon her lip did all the Graces play,
And on her breasts ten thousand Cupids lay.

Then many a doting lover came
   From seventeen till twenty-one,
Each told her of his mighty flame,
   But she, forsooth, affected none.
One was not handsome, t'other was not fine,
This of tobacco smelt, and that of wine.

But t'other day it was my fate
   To walk along that way alone,
I saw no coach before her gate,
   But at the door I heard her moan:
She dropped a tear, and sighing, seemed to say,
Young ladies, marry, marry while you may!

SIDNEY GODOLPHIN

Song

Or love mee lesse, or love mee more
 and play not with my liberty,
Either take all, or all restore,
 bind mee at least, or set mee free,
Let mee some nobler torture finde
 than of a doubtfull wavering mynd,
Take all my peace, but you betray
 myne honour too this cruell way.

Tis true that I have nurst before
 that hope of which I now complaine,
And having little sought no more,
 fearing to meet with your disdaine:
The sparks of favour you did give,
 I gently blew to make them live:
And yet have gained by all this care
 no rest in hope, nor in despaire.

I see you weare that pittying smile
 which you have still vouchsaf't my smart,
Content thus cheaply to beguile
 and entertaine an harmlesse heart:
But I no longer can give way
 to hope, which doeth so little pay,
And yet I dare no freedome owe
 whilst you are kind, though but in shew.

Then give me more, or give me lesse,
 do not disdaine a mutuall sense,
Or your unpittying beauties dresse
 in their owne free indifference;

But shew not a severer eye
sooner to give mee liberty,
For I shall love the very scorne
which for my sake you do put on.

ROBERT GOULD

Song
Wit and Beauty

When from her Beauty long I've strove
    To free my doating Heart,
Her wit brings back my fliting Love,
    And chains it down by Art.

Then, when her wit I've often foil'd,
    With one commanding view,
I'm by her Eyes again beguil'd,
    And captive took anew.

Her Wit alone were vain, alone
    Her Beauty would not do;
But what the Devil can be done
    With Wit and Beauty too?

WILLIAM HABINGTON

To Roses in the Bosome of Castara

Yee blushing virgins happie are
In the chaste nunn'ry of her brests,
For hee'd prophane so chaste a faire,
Who ere shall call them Cupid's nests.

Transplanted thus how bright yee grow,
How rich a perfume doe yee yeeld?
In some close garden, cowslips so
Are sweeter than i'th' open field.

In those white cloysters live secure
From the rude blasts of wanton breath,
Each houre more innocent and pure,
Till you shall wither into death.

Then that which living gave you roome,
Your glorious sepulcher shall be.
There wants no marble for a tombe,
Whose brest hath marble beene to me.

The Description of Castara

Like the violet which alone
Prospers in some happy shade:
My Castara lives unknowne,
To no looser eye betray'd,
   For shee's to her selfe untrue,
   Who delights i'th' publicke view.

Such is her beauty, as no arts
Have enricht with borrowed grace.
Her high birth no pride imparts,
For she blushes in her place.
    Folly boasts a glorious blood,
    She is noblest being good.

Cautious she knew never yet
What a wanton courtship meant;
Not speaks loud to boast her wit,
In her silence eloquent.
    Of her self survey she takes,
    But 'tweene men no difference makes.

She obeyes with speedy will
Her grave parents' wise commands.
And so innocent, that ill,
She nor acts, nor understands.
    Women's feet runne still astray,
    If once to ill they know the way.

She sailes by that rocke, the court,
Where oft honour splits her mast:
And retir'dnesse thinks the port,
Where her fame may anchor cast.
    Vertue safely cannot sit,
    Where vice is enthron'd for wit.

She holds that daye's pleasure best,
Where sinne waits not on delight,
Without maske, or ball, or feast,
Sweetly spends a winter's night.
    O're that darknesse, whence is thrust,
    Prayer and sleepe oft governs lust.

She her throne makes reason climbe,
While wild passions captive lie.
And each article of time,
Her pure thoughts to Heaven flie:
　All her vowes religious be,
　And her love she vowes to me.

To Castara
The Reward of Innocent Love

We saw and woo'd each other's eyes,
My soule contracted then with thine,
And both burnt in one sacrifice,
By which our marriage grew divine.

Let wilder youth, whose soule is sense,
Prophane the temple of delight,
And purchase endlesse penitence,
With the stolne pleasure of one night.

Time's ever ours, while we despise
The sensuall idol of our clay,
For though the Sunne doe set and rise,
We joy one everlasting day.

Whose light no jealous clouds obscure,
While each of us shine innocent,
The troubled stream is still impure,
With vertue flies away content.

And though opinions often erre,
Wee'le court the modest smile of fame,
For sinne's blacke danger circles her,
Who hath infection in her name.

Thus when to one darke silent roome,
Death shall our loving coffins thrust:
Fame will build columnes on our tombe,
And adde a perfume to our dust.

(Fine Young Folly)

Fine young Folly, though you wear
    That fair Beauty, I did swear,
Yet you ne'er could reach my heart,
For we courtiers learn at school
Only with your sex to fool,
You're not worth our serious part.

When I sigh and kiss your hand,
Crosse mine Armes, and wondring stand,
    Holding fairly with your eye:
Then dilate on my desires,
Swear the Sun ne'er shot such fires,
    All is but a handsome lye.

When I eye your Curles or Lace,
Gentle soul, you think your face
    Straight some murder doth commit;
And your conscience doth begin
To be scrup'lous of my sin,
When I court to shew my wit.

Wherefore Madam, wear no cloud,
Nor to check my flames grow proud;
    For in sooth I much do doubt,
'Tis the powder in your hair,
Not your breath perfumes the Air,
And your clothes that set you out.

Yet though truth hath this confest,
And I swear I love in jest,
    Courteous soul, when next I court,
And protest an amorous flame,
You'll vow, I in earnest am;
    Bedlam, this is pretty sport.

ROBERT HEATH

On Clarastella Walking in Her Garden

See how *Flora* smiles to see
This approaching Deitie!
Where each herb looks young and green
In presence of their coming Queen!
Ceres with all her fragrant store,
Could never boast so sweet a flow'r;
While thus in triumph she doth go
The greater Goddess of the two.
Here the Violet bows to greet
Her with homage to her feet;
There the Lilly pales with white
Got by her reflexed light;
Here a Rose in crimson dye
Blushes through her modestie;
There a Pansie hangs his head
'Bout to shrink into his bed,
'Cause so quickly she pass'd by
Not returning suddenly;
Here the Currants red and white
In yon green bush at her sight
Peep through their shady leaves, and cry
Come eat me, as she passes by;
There a bed of Camomile,
When she presseth it doth smell
More fragrant than the perfum'd East,
Or the *Phoenix* spicie nest;
Here the Pinks in rowes do throng
To guard her as she walks along.
There the flexive Turnsole bends
Guided by the rayes she sends
From her bright eyes, as if thence

It suckt life by influence;
Whilst She the prime and chiefest flow'r
In all the Garden by her pow'r
And onely life-inspiring breath
Like the warm Sun redeems from death
Their drooping heads, and bids them live
To tell us She their sweets did give.

Song in a Siege

Fill, fill the goblet full with sack!
I mean our tall black-jerkin Jack,
Whose hide is proof 'gainst rabble-Rout,
And will keep all ill weathers out.
What though our plate be coin'd and spent?
Our faces next we'll send to the mint:
And 'fore we'll basely yield the town,
Sack it our selves and drink it down.

Accurst be he doth talk or think
Of treating, or denies to drink,
Such drie hopsucking narrow souls
Taste not the freedome of our bowles.
They only are besieg'd, whilst we
By drinking purchase libertie.
Wine doth enlarge, and ease our minds,
Who freely drinks no thraldome finds.

Let's drink then as we us'd to fight,
As long as we can stand, in spight
Of Foe or Fortune! who can tell?
She with our cups again may swell;
He neither dares to die nor fight,
Whom harmless fears from healths affright:
Then let us drink our sorrows down,
And ourselves up to keep the town.

ROBERT HERRICK

His Prayer to Ben. Johnson

When I a Verse shall make,
Know I have praid thee,
For old *Religions* sake,
Saint *Ben* to aide me.

2   Make the way smooth for me,
When I, thy *Herrick*,
Honouring thee, on my knee
Offer my *Lyrick*.

3   Candles Ile give to thee,
And a new Altar;
And thou Saint *Ben*, shalt be
Writ in my *Psalter*.

A Short Hymne to Venus

Goddesse, I do love a Girle
   Rubie-lipt, and tooth'd with *Pearl*
If so be, I may but prove
Luckie in this Maide I love:
I will promise there shall be
Mirtles offer'd up to Thee.

To Anthea,
Who May Command Him Any Thing

Bid me to live, and I will live
   Thy Protestant to be:

Or bid me love, and I will give
    A loving heart to thee.

2 A heart as soft, a heart as kind,
    A heart as sound and free,
  As in the whole world thou canst find,
    That heart Ile give to thee.

3 Bid that heart stay, and it will stay,
    To honour thy Decree:
  Or bid it languish quite away,
    And't shall doe so for thee.

4 Bid me to weep, and I will weep,
    While I have eyes to see:
  And having none, yet I will keep
    A heart to weep for thee.

5 Bid me despaire, and Ile despaire,
    Under that *Cypresse* tree:
  Or bid me die, and I will dare
    E'en Death, to die for thee.

6 Thou art my life, my love, my heart,
    The very eyes of me:
  And hast command of every part,
    To live and die for thee.

How Roses came Red

1 Roses at first were white,
    Till they co'd not agree,
  Whether my *Sapho's* breast,
    Or they more white sho'd be.

2   But being vanquisht quite,
       A blush their cheeks bespred;
    Since which (beleeve the rest)
       The *Roses* first came red.

To the *Virgins*, to make much of *Time*

1   Gather ye Rose-buds while ye may,
       Old Time is still a flying:
    And this same flower that smiles to day,
       To morrow will be dying.

2   The glorious Lamp of Heaven, the Sun,
       The higher he's a getting;
    The sooner will his Race be run,
       And neerer he's to Setting.

3   That Age is best, which is the first,
       When Youth and Blood are warmer;
    But being spent, the worse, and worst
       Times, still succeed the former.

4   Then be not coy, but use your time;
       And while ye may, goe marry:
    For having lost but once your prime,
       You may for ever tarry.

The *Frozen Heart*

I freeze, I freeze, and nothing dwels
In me but Snow, and *ysicles*.
For pitties sake give your advice,

To melt this snow, and thaw this ice;
I'le drink down Flames, but if so be
Nothing but love can supple me;
I'le rather keepe this frost, and snow,
Then to be thaw'd, or heated so.

The Vine

I dream'd this mortal part of mine
Was Metamorphoz'd to a Vine;
Which crawling one and every way,
Enthrall'd my dainty *Lucia*.
Me thought, her long small legs & thighs
I with my *Tendrils* did surprize;
Her Belly, Buttocks, and her Waste
By my soft *Nerv'lits* were embrac'd:
About her head I writhing hung,
And with rich clusters (hid among
The leaves) her temples I behung
So that my *Lucia* seem'd to me
Young *Bacchus* ravisht by his tree.
My curles about her neck did craule,
And armes and hands they did enthrall:
So that she could not freely stir,
(All parts there made one prisoner.)
But when I crept with leaves to hide
Those parts, which maids keep unespy'd,
Such fleeting pleasures there I took,
That with the fancie I awook;
And found (Ah me!) this flesh of mine
More like a *Stock*, then like a *Vine*.

Cherrie-Ripe

Cherrie-Ripe, Ripe, Ripe, I cry,
   Full and faire ones; come and buy:
If so be, you ask me where
They doe grow? I answer, There,
Where my *Julia's* lips doe smile;
There's the Land, or Cherry-Ile:
Whose Plantations fully show
All the yeere, where Cherries grow.

Delight in Disorder

A sweet disorder in the dresse
   Kindles in cloathes a wantonnesse:
A Lawne about the shoulders thrown
Into a fine distraction:
An erring Lace, which here and there
Enthralls the Crimson Stomacher:
A Cuffe neglectfull, and thereby
Ribbands to flow confusedly:
A winning wave (deserving Note)
In the tempestuous petticote;
A carelesse shooe-string, in whose tye
I see a wilde civility:
Doe more bewitch me, then when Art
Is too precise in every part.

Divination by a Daffadill

When a daffadill I see,
   Hanging down his head t'wards me

Guesse I may, what I must be:
First, I shall decline my head;
Secondly, I shall be dead;
Lastly, safely buryed.

The Suspition upon His Over-much Familiarity with a Gentlewoman

And must we part, because some say,
　　Loud is our love, and loose our play,
And more then well becomes the day?
Alas for pitty! and for us
Most innocent, and injur'd thus.
Had we kept close, or play'd within,
Suspition now had been the sinne,
And shame had follow'd long ere this,
T'ave plagu'd, what now unpunisht is.
But we as fearlesse of the Sunne,
As faultlesse; will not wish undone,
What now is done: since *where no sin
Unbolts the doore, no shame comes in.*
Then comely and most fragrant Maid,
Be you more warie, then afraid
Of these Reports; because you see
The fairest most suspected be.
The common formes have no one eye,
Or eare of burning jealousie
To follow them: but chiefly, where
Love makes the cheek, and chin a sphere
To dance and play in: (Trust me) there
Suspicion questions every haire.
Come, you are faire; and sho'd be seen
While you are in your sprightfull green:
And what though you had been embrac't

By me, were you for that unchast?
No, no, no more then is yond' Moone,
Which shining in her perfect Noone;
In all that great and glorious light,
Continues cold, as is the night.
Then, beauteous Maid, you may retire;
And as for me, my chast desire
Shall move t'wards you; although I see
Your face no more: So live you free
From Fames black lips, as you from me.

Upon a Wife that Dyed Mad with Jealousie

In this little Vault she lyes,
   Here, with all her jealousies:
Quiet yet; but if ye make
Any noise, they both will wake,
And such spirits raise, 'twill then
Trouble Death to lay agen.

The Cruell Maid

And Cruell Maid, because I see
You scornfull of my love, and me:
Ile trouble you no more; but goe
My way, where you shall never know
What is become of me: there I
Will find me out a path to die;
Or learne some way how to forget
You, and your name, for ever: yet
Ere I go hence; know this from me,

What will, in time, your Fortune be:
This to you coynesse I will tell;
And having spoke it once, Farewell.
The Lillie will not long endure;
Nor the Snow continue pure:
The Rose, the Violet, one day
See, both these Lady-flowers decay:
And you must fade, as well as they.
And it may chance that Love may turn,
And (like to mine) make your heart burn
And weep to see't; yet this thing doe,
That my last Vow commends to you:
When you shall see that I am dead,
For pitty let a teare be shed;
And (with your Mantle o're me cast)
Give my cold lips a kisse at last:
If twice you kisse, you need not feare,
That I shall stir, or live more here.
Next, hollow out a Tombe to cover
Me; me, the most despised Lover:
And write thereon, This, *Reader, know,*
Love kill'd this man. No more but so.

Upon a Child that Dyed

Here she lies, a pretty bud,
    Lately made of flesh and blood:
Who, as soone, fell fast asleep,
As her little eyes did peep.
Give her strewings; but not stir
The earth, that lightly covers her.

The Kisse. *A Dialogue*

1   Among thy Fancies, tell me this,
       What is the thing we call a kisse?
2   I shall resolve ye, what it is.

       It is a creature born and bred
       Between the lips, (all cherrie-red,)
       By love and warme desires fed,
Chor. And makes more soft the Bridall Bed.

2   It is an active flame, that flies,
       First, to the Babies of the eyes;
       And charmes them there with lullabies;
Chor. And stils the Bride too, when she cries.

2   Then to the chin, the cheek, the eare,
       It frisks, and flyes, now here, now there,
       'Tis now farre off, and then tis nere;
Chor. And here, and there, and every where.

1   Ha's it a speaking virtue? 2 Yes;
1   How speaks it, say? 2 Do you but this,
       Part your joyn'd lips, then speakes your kisse;
Chor. And this loves sweetest language is.

1   Has it a body? 2 I, and wings
       With thousand rare encolourings:
       And as it flyes, it gently sings,
Chor. Love, honie yeelds; but never stings.

The Poet Loves a Mistresse, But not to Marry

1 I do not love to wed,
     Though I do love to wooe;

And for a maidenhead
Ile beg, and buy it too.

2   Ile praise, and Ile approve
    Those maids that never vary;
    And fervently Ile love;
    But yet I would not marry.]

3   Ile hug, Ile kisse, Ile play,
    And Cock-like Hens Ile tread:
    And sport it any way;
    But in the Bridall Bed:

4   For why? that man is poore,
    Who hath but one of many;
    But crown'd he is with store,
    That single may have any.

5   Why then, say, what is he
    (To freedome so unknown)
    Who having two or three,
    Will be content with one?

To Phillis to Love, and Live with Him

Live, live with me, and thou shalt see
The pleasures Ile prepare for thee:
What sweets the Country can afford
Shall blesse thy Bed, and blesse thy Board.
The soft sweet Mosse shall be thy bed,
With crawling Woodbine over-spread:
By which the silver-shedding streames
Shall gently melt thee into dreames.
Thy clothing next, shall be a Gowne

Made of the Fleeces purest Downe.
The tongues of Kids shall be thy meate;
Their Milke thy drinke; and thou shalt eate
The Paste of Filberts for thy bread
With Cream of Cowslips buttered:
Thy Feasting-Tables shall be Hills
With *Daisies* spread, and *Daffadils*;
Where thou shalt sit, and *Red-brest* by,
For meat, shall give thee melody.
Ile give thee Chaines and Carkanets
Of *Primroses* and *Violets*.
A Bag and Bottle thou shalt have;
That richly wrought, and This as brave;
So that as either shall expresse
The Wearer's no meane Shepheardesse.
At Sheering-times, and yearely Wakes,
When *Themilis* his pastime makes,
There thou shalt be; and be the wit,
Nay more, the Feast, and grace of it.
On Holy-dayes, when Virgins meet
To dance the Heyes with nimble feet;
Thou shalt come forth, and then appeare
The *Queen of Roses* for that yeere.
And having danc't ('bove all the best)
Carry the Garland from the rest.
In Wicker-baskets Maids shal bring
To thee (my dearest Shephardling)
The blushing Apple, bashfull Peare,
And shame-fac't Plum, (all simp'ring there).
Walk in the Groves, and thou shalt find
The name of *Philis* in the Rind
Of every straight, and smooth-skin tree;
Where kissing that, Ile twice kisse thee.
To thee, a Sheep-hook I will send,
Be-pranckt with Ribbands, to this end,
This, this alluring Hook might be

Lesse for to catch a sheep, then me.
Thou shalt have Possets, Wassails fine,
Not made of Ale, but spiced Wine;
To make thy Maids and selfe free mirth,
All sitting neer the glitt'ring Hearth.
Thou sha't have Ribbands, Roses, Rings,
Gloves, Garters, Stockings, Shooes, and Strings
Of winning Colours, that shall move
Others to Lust, but me to Love.
These (nay) and more, thine own shal be,
If thou wilt love, and live with me.

To Electra

I dare not ask a kisse;
   I dare not beg a smile;
Lest having that, or this,
   I might grow proud the while.

No, no, the utmost share
   Of my desire, shall be
Onely to kisse that Aire,
   That lately kissed thee.

Love Dislikes Nothing

Whatsoever thing I see,
Rich or poore although it be;
'Tis a Mistresse unto mee.

Be my Girle, or faire or browne,
Do's she smile, or do's she frowne:
Still I write a Sweet-heart downe.

Be she rough, or smooth of skin;
When I touch, I then begin
For to let Affection in.

Be she bald, or do's she weare
Locks incurl'd of other haire;
I shall find enchantment there.

Be she whole, or be she rent,
So my fancie be content,
She's to me most excellent.

Be she fat, or be she leane,
Be she sluttish, be she cleane,
I'm a man for ev'ry Sceane.

Upon Prew His Maid

In this little Urne is laid
Prewdence Baldwin (once my maid)
From whose happy spark here let
Spring the purple Violet.

Another Grace for a Child

Here a little child I stand,
Heaving up my either hand;
Cold as Paddocks though they be,
Here I lift them up to Thee,
For a Benizon to fall
On our meat, and on us all.   *Amen.*

THOMAS HEYRICK

Martial

Dost think He whom thy liberal Table drew,
Can ever be to Love or Friendship true?
He loves thy Mullets, Oysters, and not Thee:
Could I so entertain him, hee'd love Me.

SIR ROBERT HOWARD

To the Unconstant Cynthia. A Song

Tell me once, Dear, how it does prove
    That I so much forsworn could be?
    I never swore always to love,
I onely vow'd still to love thee:
    And art thou now what thou wert then,
    Unsworn unto by other men?

In thy fair Breast, and once-fair Soul,
I thought my Vows were writ alone;
But others' Oaths so blurr'd the Scrole,
That I no more could read my own.
    And am I still oblig'd to pay
    When you had thrown the Bond away?

Nor must we onely part in Joy,
Our tears as well must be unkind:
Weep you, that could such truth destroy,
And I, that could such falseness find.
    Thus we must unconcern'd remain
    In our divided Joys and Pain.

Yet we may love, but on this diff'rent score,
You what I am, I what you were before.

PATHERICKE JENKYN

Love and Respect

It is not that I love thee, fairest,
   Less than when my love I tender'd,
But 'twas hopeless love, my dearest,
   That my deep affection hinder'd.

Yet 'tis not hopeless love shall fear me,
   Or command my love to end,
'Tis the high respect I bear thee,
   Will not leave me to offend.

Were I confident to carry
   Thy affection, it would be
No content at all to marry
   If the conquest were not free.

But if you vouchsafe to pardon
   My presumption, do but prove,
I will render thee the guerdon
   Of a never-dying love.

HENRY KING

Sonnet

Tell mee no more how faire shee is;
    I have no mind to heare
The Story of that distant Blisse
    I never shall come neere.
By sad experience I have found
That Hir perfection is my wound.

And tell mee not how fond I am
    To tempt a daring Fate,
From whence no triumph ever came
    But to repent too late.
There is some hope ere long I may
In silence dote my self away.

I aske no Pitty (Love!) from thee,
    Nor will thy Justice blame;
So that thou wilt not envy mee
    The glory of my Flame:
Which crownes my Heart, when e're it dyes,
In that it falles Hir Sacrifice.

The Farwell

Farwell fond Love, under whose childish whipp
I have serv'd out a weary prentishipp;
Thou that hast made mee thy scorn'd property,
To dote on Rocks, but yielding Loves to fly:
Go bane of my dear quiet and content,
Mow practise on some other Patient.

Farwell false Hope, that fann'd my warme desire
Till it had rais'd a wild unruly fire,
Which nor Sighes coole, nor teares extinguish can,
Allthough my Eyes out-flow'd the Ocean:
Forth of my thoughts for ever, Thing of Aire,
Begun in Errour, finish't in Despaire.

Farwell vaine World, upon whose restless Stage
Twixt Love and Hope I have fool'd out my Age;
Henceforth, ere sue to thee for my redresse,
I'le wooe the Wind, or court the Wildernesse,
And buryed from the Daye's discovery,
Study a slow, yet certaine way to Dy.

My wofull Monument shall be a Cell,
The murmur of the purling brook my Knell.
My lasting Epitaph the Rock shall groane:
Thus when sad Lovers ask the weeping Stone,
What wretched thing does in that Center ly?
The hollow Eccho will reply, 'Twas I.

Madam Gabrina, or the Ill-Favourd Choice

I have oft wondred, why Thou didst elect
Thy Mistris of a stuff none could affect
That wore his Eyes in the right place. A Thing
Made up, when Nature's powers lay slumbering.
One, where all pregnant imperfections mett
To make hir Sexe's scandall: Teeth of Jett,
Haire dy'd in Orpment, from whose fretfull hue
Canidia her highest witchcrafts drew:
A Lipp most Thin and Pale, But such a Mouth
Which, like the Poles, is stretched North and South:
A Face so colour'd, and of such a forme,

As might defyance bidd unto a Storme:
And the complexion of her sallow hide
Like a wrack't Body wash't up by the Tide:
Eyes small: A Nose so to hir Vizard glew'd
As if 'twould take a Plannet's Altitude:
Last, for her Breath; 'tis somewhat like the smell
That does in Ember-weekes on Fishstreet dwell:
Or as a man should fasting sent the Rose
Which in the savoury Bear-garden growes.
If a Fox cures the Paralyticall,
Hadst thou ten Palseys, shee'd out-stink them all.

But I have found thy plott: sure thou didst try
To put Thyself past Hope of Jealousy:
And whilst unlearned Fooles their Senses please,
Thou cur'st thy Appetite by a Disease;
As many use, to kill an Itch withall,
Quicksilver, or some biting Minerall.

Dote upon handsome things each common man
With little study and lesse labour can:
But to make Love to a Deformity,
Only commends thy great ability,
Who from hard-favour'd Objects drawst content,
As Estriches from Iron nutriment.

Well take hir, and like mounted George, in bed
Boldly atchieve thy Dragon's mayden-head:
Where (though scarce sleep) thou may'st Rest, confident
None dares beguile thee of thy Punishment.
The sinne were not more foule he should committ,
Then is that Shee, with whom he acted it.

Yet take this comfort. When old age shall raze
Or Sicknes ruine many a good Face,
Thy choice cannot impaire, No cunning curse
Can mend that Night-peece: That is, Make her worse.

SIR FRANCIS KYNASTON

To Cynthia. On Concealment of Her Beauty

Do not conceale thy radiant eyes,
The starre-light of serenest skies,
Lest wanting of their heavenly light,
They turne to *Chaos* endlesse night.

Do not conceale those tresses faire,
The silken snares of thy curl'd haire,
Lest finding neither gold, nor Ore,
The curious Silke-worm worke no more.

Do not conceale those breasts of thine,
More snowe white than the Apenine,
Lest if there be like cold or frost,
The Lilly be for ever lost.

Do not conceale that fragrant scent,
Thy breath, which to all flowers hath lent
Perfumes, lest it being supprest,
No spices growe in all the East.

Do not conceale thy heavenly voice,
Which makes the hearts of gods rejoyce,
Lest Musicke hearing no such thing,
The Nightingale forget to sing.

Do not conceale, not yet eclipse
Thy pearly teeth with Corrall lips,
Lest that the Seas cease to bring forth
Gems, which from thee have all their worth.

Do not conceale no beauty, grace,
That's either in thy minde or face,
Lest vertue overcome by vice,
Make men beleeve no Paradise.

RICHARD LEIGH

Her Window

Here first the Day does break,
And for Access does seek,
Repairing for Supplies
To her now-op'ned Eyes;
Then, (with a gentle Light
Gilding the Shades of Night),
Their Cirtains drawn, does come
To draw those of her Room;
Both open, a small Ray
Does spread abroad the Day,
Which peepe into each Nest
Where neighb'ring Birds do rest;
Who, spread upon their yong,
Begin their Morning-Song,
And from their little home
Nearer her Window come,
While from low Boughs they hop
And perch upon the Top;
And so from Bough to Bough
Still singing, as they go,
In praise of Light and Her
Whom they to Light prefer;
By whose Protection blest,
So quietly they rest,
Secure as in the Wood
In such a Neighbourhood:
While undisturb'd they sit
Fearing no Hawk nor Net,
And here the first News sing
Of the approaching Spring:

The Spring which ever here
Does first of all appear;
Its fair Course still begun
By Her and by the Sun.

RICHARD LOVELACE

To Lucasta, going to the Warres

I

Tell me not (Sweet) I am unkinde,
    That from the Nunnerie
Of thy chaste breast, and quiet minde,
    To Warre and Armes I flie.

II

True; a new Mistresse now I chase,
    The first Foe in the Field;
And with a stronger Faith imbrace
    A Sword, a Horse, a Shield.

III

Yet this Inconstancy is such,
    As you too shall adore;
I could not love thee (Deare) so much,
    Lov'd I not Honour more.

The Scrutinie

I

Why should you sweare I am forsworn,
    Since thine I vow'd to be?
Lady it is already Morn,
    And 'twas last night I swore to thee
That fond impossibility.

II

Have I not lov'd thee much and long,
   A tedious twelve houres space?
I must all other Beauties wrong,
   And rob thee of a new imbrace;
Could I still dote upon thy Face.

III

Not, but all joy in thy browne haire,
   By others may be found;
But I must search the black and faire
   Like skilfull Minerallist's that sound
For Treasure in un-plow'd-up ground.

IV

Then, if when I have lov'd my round,
   Thou prov'st the pleasant she;
With spoyles of meaner Beauties crown'd,
   I laden will returne to thee,
Ev'd sated with Varietie.

Gratiana Dauncing and Singing

I

See! with what constant Motion
Even, and glorious, as the Sunne,
   Gratiana steeres that Noble Frame,
Soft as her breast, sweet as her voyce
That gave each winding Law and poyze,
   And swifter then the wings of Fame.

II

She beat·the happy Pavement
By such a Starre made Firmament,
   Which now no more the Roofe envies;
But swells up high with *Atlas* ev'n,
Bearing the brighter, nobler Heav'n,
   And in her, all the Dieties.

III

Each step trod out a Lovers thought
And the Ambitious hopes he brought,
   Chain'd to her brave feet with such arts,
Such sweet command, the gentle awe,
As when she ceas'd, we fighting saw
   The floore lay pav'd with broken hearts.

IV

So did she move; so did she sing
Like the Harmonious spheres that bring
   Unto their Rounds their musick's ayd;
Which she performed such a way,
As all th' inamour'd world will say
   The *Graces* daunced, and *Apollo* play'd.

La Bella Bona Roba

I

I Cannot tell who loves the Skeleton
Of a poor Marmoset, nought but boan, boan.
Give me a nakednesse with her cloath's on.

II

Such whose white-sattin upper coat of skin,
Cut upon Velvet rich Incarnadin,
Ha's yet a Body (and of Flesh) within.

III

Sure it is meant good Husbandry in men,
Who do incorporate with Aery leane,
T'repair their sides, and get their Ribb agen.

IV

Hard hap unto that Huntsman that Decrees
Fat joys for all his swet, when as he sees,
After his 'Say, nought but his Keepers Sees.

V

Then Love I beg, when next thou tak'st thy Bow,
Thy angry shafts, and dost Heart-chasing go,
Passe *Rascall Deare*, strike me the largest Doe.

A Loose Saraband

I

Nay, prethee Dear, draw nigher,
    Yet closer, nigher yet;
Here is a double Fire,
    A dry one and a wet:
True lasting Heavenly Fuel
Puts out the Vestal jewel,
When once we twining marry
Mad Love with wilde Canary.

2

Off with that crowned Venice
   'Till all the House doth flame,
Wee'l quench it straight in Rhenish,
   Or what we must not name:
Milk lightning still asswageth,
So when our fury rageth,
As th' only means to cross it,
Wee'l drown it in Love's posset.

3

Love never was Well-willer,
   Unto my Nag or mee,
Ne'er watter'd us ith' Cellar,
   But the cheap Buttery:
At th' head of his own Barrells,
Where broach'd are all his Quarrels,
Should a true noble Master
Still make his Guest his Taster.

4

See all the World how't staggers,
   More ugly drunk then we,
As if far gon in daggers,
   And blood it seem'd to be:
We drink our glass of Roses,
Which nought but sweet disclosures,
Then in our Loyal Chamber,
Refresh us with Loves Amber.

5

Now tell me, thou fair Cripple,
   That dumb canst scarcely see

Th' almightinesse of Tipple,
    And th' ods 'twixt thee and thee:
What of Elizium's missing?
Still Drinking and still Kissing;
Adoring plump *October*;
Lord! what is Man and Sober?

6

Now, is there such a Trifle
    As Honour, the fools Gyant?
What is there left to rifle,
    When Wine makes all parts plyant?
Let others Glory follow,
In their false riches wallow,
And with their grief be merry;
Leave me but Love and Sherry.

To *Althea, from Prison*

I

When Love with unconfined wings
    Hovers within my Gates;
And my divine *Althea* brings
    To whisper at the Grates:
When I lye tangled in her haire,
    And fettered to her eye;
The *Gods* that wanton in the Aire,
    Know no such Liberty.

II

When flowing Cups run swiftly round
    With no allaying *Thames*,

Our carelesse heads with Roses bound,
    Our hearts with Loyall Flames;
When thirsty griefe in Wine we steepe,
    When Healths and draughts go free,
Fishes that tipple in the Deepe,
    Know no such Libertie.

III

When (like committed Linnets) I
    With shriller throat shall sing
The sweetness, Mercy, Majesty,
    And glories of my KING;
When I shall voyce aloud, how Good
    He is, how Great should be;
        Inlarged Winds that curle the Flood,
        Know no such Liberty.

IV

Stone Walls doe not a Prison make,
    Nor I'ron bars a Cage;
Mindes innocent and quiet take
    That for an Hermitage;
If I have freedome in my Love,
    And in my soule am free;
Angels alone that Sore above,
    Injoy such Liberty.

Love *Made in the First Age: To Chloris*

I

In the Nativity of time,
    Chloris! it was not thought a Crime
    In direct *Hebrew* for to woe.

Now wee make Love, as all on fire,
Ring Retrograde our lowd Desire,
   And court in *English* Backward too.

2

Thrice happy was that golden Age,
When Complement was constru'd Rage,
   And fine words in the Center hid;
When cursed *No* stain'd no Maids Blisse,
And all discourse was summ'd in *Yes*,
   And Nought forbad, but to forbid.

3

Love then unstinted, Love did sip,
And cherries pluck'd fresh from the Lip,
   On Cheeks and Roses free he fed;
Lasses like *Autumne* Plums did drop,
And Lads, indifferently did crop
   A Flower, and a Maiden-head.

4

Then unconfined each did Tipple
Wine from the Bunch, Milk from the Nipple,
   Paps tractable as Udders were;
Then equally the wholsome Jellies,
Were squeez'd from Olive-Trees, and Bellies,
   Nor Suits of Trespasse did they fear.

5

A fragrant Bank of Straw-berries,
Diaper'd with Violets Lyes,
   Was Table, Table-cloth, and Fare;

No Pallace to the Clouds did swell,
Each humble Princesse then did dwell
   In the *Piazza* of her Hair.

6

Both broken Faith, and th' cause of it,
All damning Gold was damm'd to th' Pit;
   Their Troth seal'd with a Clasp and Kisse,
Lasted untill that extreem day,
In which they smil'd their Souls away,
   And in each other breath'd new blisse.

7

Because no fault, there was no tear;
No grone did grate the granting Ear;
   No false foul breath their Del'cat smell:
No Serpent kiss poyson'd the Fast,
Each touch was naturally Chast,
   And their mere Sense a Miracle.

8

Naked as their own innocence,
And unimbroyder'd from Offence
   They went, above poor Riches, gay;
On softer than the Cignets Down,
In beds they tumbled of their own;
   For each within the other lay.

9

Thus did they live: Thus did they love,
Repeating only joyes Above;
   And Angels were, but with Cloaths on,

Which they would put off cheerfully,
To bathe them in the *Galaxie*,
   Then gird them with the Heavenly Zone.

10

Now, CHLORIS! miserably crave,
The offer'd blisse you would not have;
   Which evermore I must deny,
Whilst ravish'd with these Noble Dreams,
And crowned with mine own soft Beams,
   Injoying of my self I lye.

ANDREW MARVELL

The Fair Singer

I

To make a final conquest of all me,
Love did compose so sweet an Enemy,
In whom both Beauties to my death agree,
Joyning themselves in fatal Harmony;
That while she with her Eyes my Heart does bind,
She with her Voice might captivate my Mind.

II

I could have fled from One but singly fair:
My dis-intangled Soul it self might save,
Breaking the curled trammels of her hair.
But how should I avoid to be her Slave,
Whose subtile Art invisibly can wreath
My Fetters of the very Air I breath?

III

It had been easie fighting in some plain,
Where Victory might hang in equal choice,
But all resistance against her is vain,
Who has th'advantage both of Eyes and Voice,
And all my Forces needs must be undone,
She having gained both the Wind and Sun.

The Mower's Song

I

My Mind was once the true survey
Of all these Medows fresh and gay;

And in the greenness of the Grass
Did see its Hopes as in a Glass;
When *Juliana* came, and She
What I do to the Grass, does to my Thoughts and Me.

II

But these, while I with Sorrow pine,
Grew more luxuriant still and fine;
That not one Blade of Grass you spy'd,
But had a Flower on either side;
When *Juliana* came, and She
What I do to the Grass, does to my Thoughts and Me.

III

Unthankful Medows, could you so
A fellowship so true forego,
And in your gawdy May-games meet,
While I lay trodden under feet?
When *Juliana* came, and She
What I do to the Grass, does to my Thoughts and Me.

IV

But what you in Compassion ought,
Shall now by my Revenge be wrought:
And Flow'rs, and Grass, and I and all,
Will in one common Ruine fall.
For *Juliana* comes, and She
What I do to the Grass, does to my Thoughts and Me.

V

And thus, ye Meadows, which have been
Companions of my thoughts more green,

Shall now the Heraldry become
With which I shall adorn my Tomb;
For *Juliana* comes, and She
What I do to the Grass, does to my Thoughts and Me.

Ametas and Thestylis Making Hay-Ropes

I

Ametas

Think'st Thou that this Love can stand,
Whilst Thou still dost say me nay?
Love unpaid does soon disband:
Love binds Love as Hay binds Hay.

II

Thestylis

Think'st Thou that this Rope would twine
If we both should turn one way?
Where both parties so combine,
Neither Love will twist nor Hay.

III

Ametas

Thus you vain Excuses find,
Which your selve and us delay:
And Love tyes a Womans Mind
Looser then with Ropes of Hay.

IV

Thestylis

What you cannot constant hope
Must be taken as you may.

V

Ametas

Then let's both lay by our Rope,
And go kiss within the Hay.

To His Coy Mistress

Had we but World enough, and Time,
This coyness Lady were no crime.
We would sit down, and think which way
To walk, and pass our long Loves Day.
Thou by the *Indian Ganges* side
Should'st Rubies find: I by the Tide
Of *Humber* would complain. I would
Love you ten years before the Flood:
And you should if you please refuse
Till the Conversion of the *Jews*.
My vegetable Love should grow
Vaster then Empires, and more slow.
An hundred years should go to praise
Thine Eyes, and on thy Forehead Gaze.
Two hundred to adore each Breast:
But thirty thousand to the rest.
An Age at least to every part,
And the last Age should show your Heart.
For Lady you deserve this State;
Nor would I love at lower rate.
    But at my back I alwaies hear
Times winged Charriot hurrying near:
And yonder all before us lye
Desarts of vast Eternity.
Thy Beauty shall no more be found;
Nor, in thy marble Vault, shall sound

My echoing Song: then Worms shall try
That long preserv'd Virginity:
And your quaint Honour turn to dust;
And into ashes all my Lust.
The Grave's a fine and private place,
But none I think do there embrace.

   Now therefore, while the youthful hew
Sits on thy skin like morning dew,
And while thy willing Soul transpires
And every pore with instant Fires,
Now let us sport us while we may;
And now, like am'rous birds of prey,
Rather at once our Time devour,
Than languish in his slow-chapt pow'r.
Let us roll all our Strength, and all
Our sweetness, up into one Ball:
And tear our Pleasures with rough strife,
Thorough the Iron gates of Life.
Thus, though we cannot make our Sun
Stand still, yet we will make him run.

An Epitaph Upon ——

Enough: and leave the rest to Fame.
'Tis to commend her but to name.
Courtship, which living she declin'd,
When dead to offer were unkind.
Where never any could speak ill,
Who would officious Praises spill?
Nor can the truest Wit or Friend,
Without Detracting, her commend.
To say she liv'd a *Virgin* chast,
In this Age loose and all unlac't;
Nor was, when Vice is so allow'd,

Of *Virtue* or asham'd, or proud;
That her Soul was on *Heaven* so bent
No Minute but it came and went;
That ready her last Debt to pay
She summ'd her Life up ev'ry day;
Modest as Morn; as Mid-day bright;
Gentle as Ev'ning; cool as Night;
'Tis true: but all so weakly said;
'Twere more Significant, *She's Dead*.

JOHN MILTON

An Epitaph on the Marchioness of Winchester

This rich Marble doth enter
The honour'd Wife of *Winchester*,
A Vicounts daughter, an Earls heir,
Besides what her vertues fair
Added to her noble birth,
More than she could own from Earth.
Summers three times eight save one
She had told, alas too soon,
After so short time of breath,
To house with darknes, and with death.
Yet had the number of her days
Bin as compleat as was her praise,
Nature and fate had had no strife
In giving limit to her life.
Her high birth, and her graces sweet,
Quickly found a lover meet;
The Virgin quire for her request
The God that sits at marriage feast;
He at their invoking came
But with a scarce-wel-lighted flame;
And in his Garland as he stood,
Ye might discern a Cypress bud.
Once had the early Matrons run
To greet her of a lovely son,
And now with second hope she goes,
And calls *Lucina* to her throws;
But whether by mischance or blame
Atropos for *Lucina* came;
And with remorsless cruelty,
Spoil'd at once both fruit and tree:
The hapless Babe before his birth

Had burial, yet not laid in earth,
And the languisht Mothers Womb
Was not long a living Tomb.
So have I seen som tender slip
Sav'd with care from Winters nip,
The pride of her carnation train,
Pluck't up by som unheedy swain,
Who onely thought to crop the flowr
New shot up from vernall showr;
But the fair blossom hangs the head
Side-ways as on a dying bed,
And those Pearls of dew she wears,
Prove to be presaging tears
Which the sad morn had let fall
On her hast'ning funerall.
Gentle Lady may thy grave
Peace and quiet ever have;
After this thy travail sore
Sweet rest sease thee evermore,
That to give the world encrease,
Shortned hast thy own lives lease;
Here besides the sorrowing
That thy noble House doth bring,
Here be tears of perfect moan
Weept for thee in *Helicon*
And som Flowers, and som Bays,
For thy Hearse to strew the ways,
Sent thee from the banks of *Came*
Devoted to thy vertuous name;
Whilst thou bright Saint high sit'st in glory,
Next her much like to thee in story,
That fair *Syrian* Shepherdess,
Who after yeers of barrenness,
The highly favour'd *Joseph* bore
To him that serv'd for her before,
And at her next birth much like thee,

Through pangs fled to felicity,
Far within the boosom bright
Of blazing Majesty and Light,
There with thee, new welcom Saint,
Like fortunes may her soul acquaint,
With thee there clad in radiant sheen,
No Marchioness, but now a Queen.

MARY MOLLINEUX

Solitude

How sweet is harmless solitude!
  What can its joys control?
Tumults and noise may not intrude,
  To interrupt the soul,

That here enjoys itself, retired
  From earth's seducing charms;
Leaving her pomp to be admired
  By such as court their harms.

While she, on contemplation's wings
  Soars far beyond the sky,
And feeds her thoughts on heavenly things
  Which in her bosom lie.

Great privileges here of old
  The wise men did obtain;
And treasure far surpassing gold
  They digged for not in vain.

The tincture of philosophers
  Here happily they found;
The music of the morning stars
  Here in their hearts did sound.

JAMES GRAHAM
MARQUIS OF MONTROSE

(My Dear and Only Love)

My dear and only Love, I pray
    This noble World of thee,
Be govern'd by no other Sway
    But purest Monarchie.
For if Confusion have a Part,
    Which vertuous Souls abhor,
And hold a Synod in thy Heart,
    I'll never love thee more.

Like *Alexander* I will reign,
    And I will reign alone,
My Thoughts shall evermore disdain
    A Rival on my Throne.
He either fears his Fate too much,
    Or his Deserts are small,
That puts it not unto the Touch,
    To win or lose it all.

But I must rule and govern still,
    And always give the Law,
And have each Subject at my Will,
    And all to stand in awe.
But 'gainst my Battery if I find
    Thou shun'st the Prize so sore,
As that thou set'st me up a Blind,
    I'll never love thee more.

Or in the Empire of thy Heart,
    Where I should solely be,

Another do pretend a Part,
  And dares to Vie with me,
Or if Committees thou erect,
  And goes on such a Score,
I'll sing and laugh at thy Neglect,
  And never love thee more.

But if thou wilt be constant then,
  And faithful of thy Word,
I'll make thee glorious by my Pen,
  And famous by my Sword.
I'll serve thee in such noble Ways,
  Was never heard before:
I'll crown and deck thee all with Bays,
  And love thee evermore.

On Himself, upon hearing what was His Sentence

Let them bestow on ev'ry Airth a Limb;
Open all my Veins, that I may swim
To Thee my Saviour, in that Crimson Lake;
Then place my purboil'd Head upon a Stake;
Scatter my Ashes, throw them in the Air:
Lord (since Thou know'st where all these Atoms are)
I'm hopeful, once Thou'lt recollect my Dust,
And confident Thou'lt raise me with the Just.

JOHN NORRIS

The Choice

No! I shan't envy him, who'er he be
That stands upon the battlements of state;
   Stand there who will for me,
   I'd rather be secure than great.
Of being so high the pleasure is but small
But long the ruin, if I chance to fall.

Let me in some sweet shade serenely lye,
Happy in leisure and obscurity;
   Whilst others place their joys
   In popularity and noise.
Let my soft minutes glide obscurely on,
Like subterraneous streams, unheard, unknown.

Thus when my days are all in silence past
A good plain country-man I'll dye at last.
   Death cannot chuse but be
   To him a mighty misery
Who to the world was popularly known
And dies a stranger to himself alone.

The Retirement

Well, I have thought on't, and I find
This busie world is nonsense all:
I here despair to please my mind,
Her sweetest honey is so mixt with gall.
Come then, I'll try how 'tis to be alone,
Live to my self a while, and be my own.

I've try'd, and bless the happy change;
So happy, I could almost vow
Never from this retreat to range,
For sure I ne'er can be so blest as now.
From all th'allays of bliss I here am free,
I pity others, and none envy me.

Here in this shady lonely grove,
I sweetly think my hours away,
Neither with business vex'd, nor love,
Which in the world bear such tyrannick sway:
No tumults can my close apartment find,
Calm as those seats above, which know no storm nor wind.

Let plots and news embroil the State,
Pray what's that to my books and me?
Whatever be the kingdom's fate,
Here I am sure t'enjoy a monarchy.
Lord of my self, accountable to none,
Like the first man in Paradise, alone.

While the ambitious vainly sue,
And of the partial stars complain,
I stand upon the shore and view
The mighty labours of the distant main,
I'm flush'd with silent joy, and smile to see
The shafts of Fortune still drop short of me.

Th' uneasie pageantry of State,
And all the plagues of thought and sense
Are far remov'd; I'm plac'd by Fate
Out of the road of all impertinence.
Thus, tho my fleeting life runs swiftly on,
'Twill not be short, because 'tis all my own.

KATHERINE PHILIPS

To My Excellent Lucasia, on Our Friendship

I did not live until this time
    Crown'd my felicity,
When I could say without a crime,
    I am not thine, but Thee.

This carcase breath'd, and walkt, and slept,
    So that the World believ'd
There was a soul the motions kept:
    But they were all deceiv'd.

For as a watch by art is wound
    To motion, such was mine:
But never had Orinda found
    A soul till she found thine;

Which now inspires, cures and supplies,
    And guides my darkened breast:
For thou art all that I can prize,
    My Joy, my life, my Rest.

No bridegroom's nor crown-conqueror's mirth
    To mine compar'd can be:
They have but pieces of this Earth,
    I've all the World in thee.

Then let our flames still light and shine,
    And no false fear control,
As innocent as our design,
    Immortal as our soul.

An Answer to Another Persuading a Lady to Marriage

Forbear, bold youth, all's Heaven here,
    And what you do aver,
To others courtship may appear,
    'Tis sacrilege to her.

She is a public deity,
    And were 't not very odd
She should dispose herself to be
    A petty household god?

First make the sun in private shine,
    And bid the world adieu,
That so he may his beams confine
    In compliment to you.

But if of that you do despair,
    Think how you did amiss,
To strive to fix her beams which are
    More bright and large than this.

SAMUEL PORDAGE

Corydon's Complaint

Those joys that us'd to flatter me
O Phyllis when I courted thee
Under yon shady beechen tree
        To cruell grief are chang'd.

Torments my pleasure, griefs my joy,
Pains my quiet rest destroy,
Since thou'rt to Corydon grown coy,
        And from my Love estrang'd.

Did e're I your commands neglect
That thus my sute you now reject
And pay my love with disrespect,
        My kindness with disdain?

Say how I purchace may reliefe,
Or murther'd must I be by grief?
Speak that my torments may be brief;
        Give death to ease my pain.

If you are pleas'd to martyr me
Or binde me unto slavery
There is another tyranny
        That you may exercise—

Those burning flames your eyes can give
A Slave, bound by Love's Chaines I live,
Nay, without hope of a reprieve;
        Thus you may tyrannize.

Since that my words are spent in vain,
Whilst Cruel you laugh at my pain,
I at the feet of your disdain
         Will fall, and prostrate lye

Henceforth I'le banish all my pleasure,
Since you the chiefest of my Treasure,
Have heaped my Griefs beyond all Measure,
         I'le yield to destiny.

JOHN WILMOT
EARL OF ROCHESTER

Love a Woman

Love a Woman! You're an *Ass*,
    'Tis a most insipid Passion
To choose out for your Happiness
    The silliest Part of God's Creation.

Let the Porter and the Groom,
    Things designed for duty Slaves,
Drudge in fair *Aurelia's* Womb,
    To get Supplies for Age and Graves:

Farewell, Woman, I intend
    Henceforth every night to sit
With my lewd well-natured Friend,
    Drinking to engender Wit.

Upon His Drinking Bowl

Vulcan contrive me such a Cup
    As *Nestor* used of old,
Shew all thy Skill to trim it up,
    Damask it round with Gold.

Make it so large, that filled with Sack
    Up to the swelling Brim,
Vast Toasts on the delicious Lake
    Like Ships at Sea may swim.

Engrave not Battle on his Cheek,
    With War I've nought to do;

I'm none of those that took *Maestricht*,
  Nor *Yarmouth* Leaguer knew.

Let it no Names of Planets tell,
  Fixt Stars or Constellations:
For I am no Sir *Sydrophel*,
  Nor none of his Relations.

But carve thereon a spreading Vine,
  Then add two lovely Boys,
Their Limbs in amorous Folds intwine,
  The type of future Joys.

Cupid and *Bacchus* my Saints are,
  May Drink and Love still reign,
With Wine I wash away my Cares,
  And then to Love again.

Love and Life, *A Song*

All my past Life is mine no more,
  The flying Hours are gone;
Like transitory Dreams given o'er,
Whose Images are kept in store
  By Memory alone.

The time that is to come, is not;
  How can it then be mine?
The present Moment's all my Lot,
And that, as fast as it is got,
  Phillis is wholly thine.

Then talk not of Inconstancy,
  False Hearts and broken vows;

If I by Miracle can be
This live-long Minute true to thee
　　'Tis all that Heaven allows.

Insulting Beauty

Insulting Beauty, you mispend
　　These Frowns upon your Slave;
Your scorn against such Rebels bend
Who dare with Confidence pretend
That other Eyes their Hearts defend
　　From all the Charms you have.

Your conquering Eyes so partial are,
　　Or Mankind is so dull,
That while I languish in Despair
Many proud senseless Hearts declare
They find you not so killing Fair
　　To wish you Merciful.

They an inglorious Freedom boast;
　　I triumph in my Chain
Nor am I unrevenged though lost;
Nor you unpunished, though unjust;
When I alone, who love you most,
　　Am killed with your Disdain.

A Dialogue Between
Strephon and Daphne

Strephon:

Prithee now, fond Fool, give o'er;
Since my Heart is gone before,

To what purpose should I stay?
Love commands another way.

Daphne:

Perjured Swain, I knew the time
When Dissembling was your Crime.
In pity now employ that Art
Which first betrayed, to ease my Heart.

Strephon:

Women can with pleasure feign:
Men dissemble still with pain.
What advantage will it prove
If I lie, who cannot love?

Daphne:

Tell me then the reason why,
Love from Hearts in Love does fly?
Why the Bird will build a Nest
Where he ne'er intends to rest?

Strephon:

Love, like other little Boys,
Cries for Hearts, as they for Toys:
Which, when gained, in Childish Play
Wantonly are thrown away.

Daphne:

Still on Wing, or on his Knees,
Love does nothing by degrees:
Basely flying when most prized,
Meanly fawning when despised:
Flattering or insulting ever,

Generous and grateful never:
All his Joys are fleeting Dreams,
All his Woes severe Extremes.

Strephon:

Nymph, unjustly you inveigh;
Love, like us, must Fate obey.
Since 'tis Nature's Law to Change,
Constancy alone is strange.
See the Heavens in Lightnings break,
Next in Storms of Thunder speak;
'Till a kind Rain from above
Makes a Calm—so 'tis in Love.
Flames begin our first Address,
Like meeting Thunder we embrace:
Then you know the Showers that fall
Quench the Fire, and quiet all.

Daphne:

How should I these Showers forget,
'Twas so pleasant to be wet?
They killed Love, I knew it well;
I died all the while they fell.
Say at least what *Nymph* it is
Robs my Breast of so much Bliss?
If she is fair, I shall be eased,
Thro' my Ruin you'll be pleased.

Strephon:

Daphne never was so fair:
Strephon, scarcely, so sincere
Gentle, Innocent, and Free,
Ever pleased with only me.
Many Charms my Heart enthral,
But there's one above 'em all:

With aversion she does fly
Tedious, Trading *Constancy*.

Daphne:

Cruel Shepherd! I submit;
Do what Love and you think fit:
Change is Fate, and not Design;
Say you would have still been mine.

Strephon:

Nymph, I cannot: 'Tis too true,
Change has greater Charms than you:
Be, by my Example, wise,
Faith to Pleasure sacrifice.

Daphne:

Silly *Swain*, I'll have you know,
'Twas my practice long ago:
Whilst you vainly thought me true,
I was false, in scorn of you.
By my Tears, my Heart's disguise,
I thy Love and thee despise.
Womankind more Joy discovers
Making Fools, than keeping Lovers.

Song. I Promised Sylvia

I Promised *Sylvia* to be true;
Nay, out of Zeal, I swore it too
And that she might believe me more
Gave her in writing what I swore:
Nor Vows, nor Oaths can Lovers bind;

So long as blessed, so long they're kind:
'Twas in a Leaf, the Wind but blew,
Away both Leaf and Promise flew.

Song.   Phillis be Gentler

Phillis, be gentler, I advise,
   Make up for time mis-spent;
When Beauty on its Death-bed lies
   'Tis high time to repent.

Such is the Malice of your Fate
   That makes you old so soon,
Your Pleasure ever comes too late,
   How early e'er begun.

Think what a wretched thing is she
   Whose Stars contrive in spite
That Morning of her Love should be
   Her fading Beauty's Night.

Then if, to make your ruin more,
   You'll peevishly be coy,
Die with the Scandal of a Whore
   And never know the Joy.

A Song of a Young Lady
to Her Ancient Lover

Ancient Person, for whom I
All the flattering Youth defie,
Long be it e'er thou grow Old

Aching, shaking, crazy, cold.
But still continue as thou art,
Ancient Person of my Heart.

On thy withered Lips and dry,
Which like barren Furrows lie,
Brooding Kisses I will pour,
Shall thy youthful Heat restore.
Such kind Showers in Autumn fall,
And a second Spring recall:
Nor from thee will ever part,
Ancient Person of my Heart.

Thy Nobler Parts, which but to name
In our Sex would be counted shame,
By Age's frozen Grasp possessed
From their Ice shall be released:
And, soothed by my reviving Hand,
In former Warmth and Vigour stand.
All a Lover's Wish can reach
For thy Joy my Love shall teach:
And for thy Pleasure shall improve
All that Art can add to Love.
Yet still I love thee without Art,
Ancient Person of my Heart.

The Mistress.   A Song

An Age in her Embraces past,
  Would seem a Winter's Day;
Where Life and Light, with envious haste
  Are torn and snatch'd away.

But, oh! how slowly Minutes roul,
  When absent from her Eyes,

That fed my Love, which is my Soul;
    It languishes and dies.

For then no more a Soul but Shade,
    It mournfully does move;
And haunts my Breast, by Absence made
    The living Tomb of Love.

You wiser Men despise me not;
    Whose Love-sick Fancy raves,
On Shades of Souls, and Heav'n know what;
    Short Ages live in Graves.

Whene'er those wounding Eyes, so full
    Of Sweetness, you did see;
Had you not been profoundly dull,
    You had gone mad like me.

Nor censure us, You who perceive
    My best belov'd and me,
Sigh and lament, complain and grieve,
    You think we disagree,

Alas! 'tis sacred Jealousie,
    Love rais'd to an Extream;
The only Proof 'twixt them and me,
    We love, and do not dream.

Fantastick Fancies fondly move;
    And in frail Joys believe,
Taking false Pleasure for true Love;
    But Pain can ne'er deceive.

Kind jealous Doubts, tormenting Fears,
    And anxious Cares, when past,
Prove our Hearts Treasure fix'd and dear,
    And make us blest at last.

A Song

Absent from thee I languish still;
  Then ask me not, When I return?
The straying Fool 'twill plainly kill,
  To wish all Day, all Night to mourn.

Dear; from thine Arms then let me fly,
  That my fantastick Mind may prove,
The Torments it deserves to try,
  That tears my fixt Heart from my Love.

When wearied with a World of Woe,
  To thy safe Bosom I retire,
Where Love and Peace and Truth does flow,
  May I contented there expire.

Lest once more wand'ring from that Heav'n,
  I fall on some base Heart unblest;
Faithless to thee, false, unforgiven,
  And lose my everlasting Rest.

Constancy.   A Song

I cannot change, as others do,
  Though you unjustly scorn:
Since that poor Swain that Sighs for you,
  For you alone was born.
No, *Phillis*, no, your Heart to move
  A surer way I'll try:
And to revenge my slighted Love,
  Will still love on, will still love on, and die.

When, kill'd with Grief, *Amintas* lies;
   And you to mind shall call,
The sighs that now unpitied rise,
   The Tears that vainly fall.
That welcome Hour that ends this Smart,
   Will then begin your Pain;
For such a faithful tender Heart
   Can never break, can never break in vain.

Epigram

Here lies a Great and Mighty King
   Whose Promise none relies on;
He never said a Foolish Thing,
   Nor ever did a Wise one.

WENTWORTH DILLON
EARL OF ROSCOMMON

Song on a Young Lady who Sung Finely, and was Afraid of a Cold

Winter, thy cruelty extend,
Till fatal tempests swell the sea.
In vain let sinking pilots pray;
    Beneath thy yoke let Nature bend,
Let piercing frost, and lasting snow,
Through woods and fields destruction sow!

    Yet we unmov'd will sit and smile,
While you these lesser ills create,
These we can bear; but, gentle Fate,
    And thou, blest Genius of our isle,
From Winter's rage defend her voice,
At which the listening Gods rejoice.

    May that celestial sound each day
With extasy transport our souls,
Whilst all our passions it controuls,
    And kindly drives our cares away;
Let no ungentle cold destroy,
All taste we have of heavenly joy!

On the Death of a Lady's Dog

Thou, happy creature, art secure
From all the torments we endure;
Despair, ambition, jealousy,
Lost friends, nor love, disquiet thee;

A sullen prudence drew thee hence
From noise, fraud, and impertinence.
Though life essay'd the surest wile,
Gilding itself with Laura's smile;
How didst thou scorn life's meaner charms,
Thou who could'st break from Laura's arms!
Poor Cynic! still methinks I hear
Thy awful murmurs in my ear;
As when on Laura's lap you lay,
Chiding the worthless crowd away.
How fondly human passions turn!
What we then envy'd, now we mourn!

SIR CHARLES SEDLEY

(Ah Cloris! That I Now Could Sit)

Ah *Cloris!* that I now could sit
    As unconcern'd, as when
Your Infant Beauty cou'd beget
    No pleasure, nor no pain.

When I the Dawn us'd to admire,
    And prais'd the coming day;
I little thought the growing fire
    Must rake my Rest away.

Your Charms in harmless Childhood lay,
    Like metals in the mine,
Age from no face took more away,
    Than Youth conceal'd in thine.

But as your Charms insensibly
    To their perfection prest,
Fond Love as unperceiv'd did flye,
    And in my Bosom rest.

My passion with your Beauty grew,
    And *Cupid* at my heart,
Still as his mother favour'd you,
    Threw a new flaming Dart.

Each glori'd in their wanton part,
    To make a Lover he
Employ'd the utmost of his Art,
    To make a Beauty she.

Though now I slowly bend to love
    Uncertain of my Fate,
If your fair self my Chains approve,
    I shall my freedom hate.

Lovers, like dying men, may well
    At first disorder'd be,
Since none alive can truly tell
    What Fortune they must see.

A Song to Celia

Not *Celia*, that I juster am
    Or better than the rest,
For I would change each Hour like them,
    Were not my Heart at rest.

But I am ty'd to very thee,
    By every Thought I have,
Thy Face I only care to see,
    Thy Heart I only crave.

All that in Woman is ador'd,
    In thy dear selfe I find,
For the whole Sex can but afford,
    The Handsome and the Kind.

Why then should I seek farther Store,
    And still make Love anew;
When Change it self can give no more,
    'Tis easie to be true.

Song

Love still has something of the Sea,
　From whence his Mother rose;
No time his Slaves from Doubt can free,
　Nor give their Thoughts repose:

They are becalm'd in clearest Days,
　And in rough Weather tost;
They wither under cold Delays,
　Or are in Tempests lost.

One while they seem to touch the Port,
　Then straight into the Main,
Some angry Wind in cruel sport
　The Vessel drives again,

At first Disdain and Pride they fear,
　Which if they chance to 'scape,
Rivals and Falsehood soon appear
　In a more dreadful shape.

By such Degrees to Joy they come,
　And are so long withstood,
So slowly they receive the Sum,
　It hardly does them good.

'Tis cruel to prolong a Pain;
　And to defer a Joy,
Believe me, gentle *Celemene*,
　Offends the winged Boy.

An hundred thousand Oaths your Fears
　Perhaps would not remove;
And if I gaz'd a thousand Years
　I could no deeper love.

Song

Phillis is my only Joy,
    Faithless as the Winds or Seas;
Sometimes coming, sometimes coy,
    Yet she never fails to please;
        If with a Frown
        I am cast down,
        Phillis smiling,
        And beguiling,
Makes me happier than before.

Tho', alas, too late I find,
    Nothing can her Fancy fix;
Yet the Moment she is kind,
    I forgive her all her Tricks;
        Which, tho' I see,
        I can't get free;
        She deceiving,
        I believing ;
What need Lovers wish for more?

(Hears Not My Phillis, How the Birds)

Hears not my Phillis, how the birds
    Their feather'd mates salute?
They tell their passion in their words:
    Must I alone be mute?
Phillis, without frown or smile,
Sat and knotted all the while.

The God of Love in thy bright eyes
    Does like a tyrant reign;

But in thy heart a child he lies,
   Without his dart or flame.
Phillis, without frown or smile,
Sat and knotted all the while.

So many months in silence past,
   And yet in raging love,
Might well deserve one word at last
   My passion should approve.
Phillis, without frown or smile,
Sat and knotted all the while.

Must then your faithful swain expire,
   And not one look obtain,
Which he, to soothe his fond desire,
   Might pleasingly explain?
Phillis, without frown or smile,
Sat and knotted all the while.

SIR EDWARD SHERBURNE

Ice and Fire

Naked Love did to thine eye,
Chloris, once to warm him, fly;
But its subtle flame, and light,
Scorch'd his wings, and spoil'd his sight.

Forc'd from thence he went to rest
In the soft couch of thy breast:
But there met a frost so great,
As his torch extinguish'd straight.

When poor Cupid, thus (constrain'd
His cold bed to leave) complain'd;
" 'Las! what lodging'd here for me,
If all ice and fire she be."

To Ligurinus.
Horat. Carm. L. 4. OD. 10. Paraphrastice

Cruel, and fair! when this soft down
   (Thy youth's bloom) shall to bristle grow;
And these fair curls thy shoulders crown,
   Shall shed, or cover'd be with snow:

When those bright roses that adorn
   Thy cheeks shall wither quite away,
And in thy glass (now made time's scorn)
   Thou shalt thy changed face survey:

Then, ah, then! (sighing) thou'lt deplore
   Thy ill-spent youth; and wish, in vain,
'Why had I not those thoughts before?
   Or come not my first looks again?'

Love's Arithmetic

By a gentle river laid,
Thirsis to his Phillis said;
Equal to these sandy grains,
Is the number of my pains:
And the drops within their bounds
Speak the sum of all my wounds.

Phillis, who like passion burns,
Thirsis answer thus returns:
'Many, as the Earth hath leaves,
Are the griefs my heart receives;
And the stars, which Heaven inspires,
Reckon my consuming fires.'

Then the shepherd, in the pride
Of his happy love, reply'd;
'With the choristers of air
Shall our numerous joys compare;
And our mutual pleasures vie
With the Cupids in thine eye.'

Thus the willing shepherdess
Did her ready love express:
'In delights our pains shall cease,
And our war be cur'd by peace;
We will count our griefs with blisses,
Thousand torments, thousand kisses.'

JAMES SHIRLEY

To the Painter Preparing to Draw M. M. H.

Be not too forward, painter; 'tis
More for thy fame, and art, to misse
All other faces, then come neer
The Lady, that expecteth here:
Be wise, and think it lesse disgrace
To draw an Angel, then her face:
For in such formes, who is so wise
To tell thee where thy error lies?
But since all beauty (that is known)
Is in her Virgin sweetnes One,
How can it be, that painting her,
But every look should make thee erre?
But thou art resolute I see;
Yet let my fancy walk with thee:
Compose a ground more dark and sad,
Then that the early Chaos had:
And shew, to the whole Sexes shame,
Beauty was darknes till she came:
Then paint her eyes, whose active light
Shall make the former shadows bright:
And with their every beam supply
New day, to draw her picture by:
Now, if thou wilt compleat the face,
A wonder paint in every place.
    Beneath these, for her fair necks sake,
White as the Paphian Turtles, make
A pillar, whose smooth base doth show
It self lost in a mount of snow:
Her brest, the house of chast desire,
Cold, but increasing others fire.
    But how I lose (instructing thee)

Thy pencil, and my Poetry!
For when thou hast exprest all art,
As high as truth, in every part,
She can resemble at the best,
One, in her beauties silence drest,
Where thou, like a dull looker on,
Art lost, and all thy art undone:
For if she speak, new wonders rise
From her teeth, chin, lip, and eyes:
So far above that excellent
Did take thee first, thou wo't repent
To have begun, and lose i'th'end
Thy eyes with wonder how to mend.
At such a losse, here's all thy choice,
Leave off, or paint her with a voice.

The Garden

This Garden does not take my eyes,
Though here you shew how art of men
Can purchase Nature at a price
Would stock old Paradise agen.

These glories while you dote upon,
I envie not your Spring nor pride,
Nay boast the Summer all your own,
My thoughts with lesse are satisfied.

Give me a little plot of ground,
Where might I with the Sun agree,
Though every day he walk the Round,
My Garden he should seldom see.

Those Tulips that such wealth display,
To court my eye, shall lose their name,
Though now they listen, as if they
Expected I should praise their flame.

But I would see my self appear
Within the Violets drooping head,
On which a melancholy tear
The discontented Morne hath shed.

Within their budds let Roses sleep,
And virgin Lillies on their stemme,
Till sighes from Lovers glide, and creep
Into their leaves to open them.

I'th'Center of my ground compose
Of Bayes and Ewe my Summer room,
Which may so oft as I repose,
Present my Arbour, and my Tombe.

No woman here shall find me out,
Or if a chance do bring one hither,
I'll be secure, for round about
I'll moat it with my eyes foul weather.

No Bird shall live within my pale,
To charme me with their shames of Art,
Unlesse some wandring Nightingale
Come here to sing and break her heart.

Upon whose death I'le try to write
An Epitaph in some funeral stone,
So sad, and true, it may invite
My self to die, and prove mine owne.

Epitaph Inscribed on a Small Piece of Marble

No more marble let him have;
He hath treasure in his grave,
And his piety will survive,
To keep his memory alive:
A glorious nothing it would be,
To say, his tomb were rich, not he.

Epitaph on the Duke of Buckingham

Here lies the best and worst of Fate,
Two Kings delight, the peoples hate,
The Courtiers star, the Kingdoms eye,
A man to draw an Angel by.
    Fears despiser, Villiers glory,
    The Great mans volume, all times story.

(The Glories of our Blood and State)

The glories of our blood and state,
    Are shadows, not substantial things,
There is no armour against fate,
    Death lays his icy hand on Kings,
        Scepter and Crown,
        Must tumble down,
And in the dust be equal made,
With the poor crooked sithe and spade.

Some men with swords may reap the field,
    And plant fresh laurels where they kill,

But their strong nerves at last must yield,
   They tame but one another still;
      Early or late,
      They stoop to fate,
And must give up the murmuring breath,
When they pale Captives creep to death.

The Garlands wither on your brow,
   Then boast no more your mighty deeds,
Upon Deaths purple Altar now,
    See where the Victor-victim bleeds,
      Your heads must come,
      To the cold Tomb;
Onely the actions of the just
Smell sweet, and blossom in their dust.

THOMAS STANLEY

Song

When I lie burning in thine eye,
   Or freezing in thy brest,
What Martyrs, in wish'd flames that die,
   Are half so pleas'd or blest?

When thy soft accents, through mine ear
   Into my soul do fly,
What Angel would not quit his sphear,
   To hear such harmony?

Or when the Kisse thou gav'st me last
   My soul stole in its breath,
What life would sooner be embrac'd
   Then so desir'd a death?

Then think not freedom I desire,
   Or would my fetters leave,
Since Phenix-like I from this fire
   Both life and youth receave.

Song

Celinda, by what potent art
   Or unresisted charm,
Dost thou thine ear and frozen heart
   Against my passion arm?

Or by what hidden influence
   Of powers in one combin'd

Dost thou rob love of either sense,
   Made deaf as well as blind?

Sure thou, as friends, united hast
   Two distant Deities,
And scorn within thy heart has plac'd,
   And love within thine eyes.

Or those soft fetters of thy hair,
   A bondage that disdains
All liberty, do guard thine ear
   Free from all other chains.

Then my complaint how canst thou hear,
   Or I this passion fly,
Since thou imprisoned hast thine ear
   And not confin'd thine eye?

The Snow-Ball

Doris, I that could repell
All those darts about thee dwell,
And had wisely learn'd to fear,
Cause I saw a Foe so near;
I that my deaf ear did arm,
'Gainst thy voices powerful charm,
And the lightning of thine eye
Durst (by closing mine) defie,
Cannot this cold snow withstand
From the whiter of thy hand;
Thy deceit hath thus done more
Then thy open force before:
For who could suspect or fear
Treason in a face so clear,

Or the hidden fires descry
Wrapt in this cold out-side lie?
Flames might thus involv'd in ice
The deceiv'd world sacrifice;
Nature, ignorant of this
Strange Antiperistasis,
Would her falling frame admire,
That by snow were set on fire.

The Farewell

Since Fate commands me hence, and I
Must leave my soul with thee, and die,
Dear, spare one sigh, or else let fall
A tear to crown my Funeral,
That I may tell my grieved heart
Thou art unwilling we should part,
And Martyrs that imbrace the fire
Shall with lesse joy then I expire.

With this last kiss I will bequeath
My soul transfus'd into thy breath,
Whose active heat shall gently slide
Into thy breast, and there reside,
And be in spight of Fate thus blest
By this sad death of Heaven possest;
Then prove but kind, and thou shalt see
Love hath more power then Destinie.

La Belle Ennemie

I yield, dear Enemy, nor know
How to resist so fair a Foe;

Who would not thy soft yoke sustain,
And bow beneath thy easie chain,
That with a bondage blest might be
Which far transcends all liberty?
    But since I freely have resign'd
At first assault my willing mind,
Insult not o're my captiv'd heart
With too much tyrannie and art,
Lest by thy scorn thou lose the prize,
Gain'd by the power of thy bright eyes,
And thou this conquest thus shalt prove,
Though got by Beauty, kept by Love.

Loves Heretick

He whose active thoughts disdain
    To be Captive to one foe,
And would break his single chain
    Or else more would undergo;
Let him learn the art of me,
By new bondage to be free.

What tyrannick Mistresse dare
    To one beauty love confine,
Who unbounded as the aire
    All may court but none decline?
Why should we the Heart deny
As many objects as the Eye?

Wheresoe're I turn or move
    A new passion doth detain me:
Those kind beauties that do love,
    Or those proud ones that disdain me;
This frown melts, and that smile burns me;
This to tears, that ashes turns me.

Soft fresh Virgins not full blown,
 With their youthful sweetnesse take me;
Sober Matrons that have known
 Long since what these prove, awake me;
Here staid coldnesse I admire,
There the lively active fire.

She that doth by skill dispence
 Every favour she bestows,
Or the harmlesse innocence
 Which nor Court nor City knows,
Both alike my soul enflame,
That wilde beauty, and this tame,

She that wisely can adorn
 Nature with the wealth of art,
Or whose rural sweets do scorn
 Borrow'd helps to take a heart,
The vain care of that's my pleasure,
Poverty of this my treasure.

Both the wanton and the coy
 Me with equal pleasures move;
She whom I by force enjoy,
 Or who forceth me to love;
This because she'l not confesse,
That not hide, her happinesse.

She whose loosely flowing hair,
 Scatter'd like the beams o'th'Morn,
Playing with the sportive Air,
 Hides the sweets it doth adorn,
Captive in that net restrains me,
In those golden fetters chains me.

Nor doth she with power lesse bright
   My divided heart invade,
Whose soft tresses spread like Night,
   O're her shoulders a black shade;
For the star-light of her eyes
Brighter shines through those dark Skies.

Black, or fair, or tall, or low,
   I alike with all can sport;
The bold sprightly *Thais* woo,
   Or the frozen Vestal Court;
Every beauty takes my minde,
Tied to all, to none confin'd.

MATTHEW STEVENSON

Song

Should I sigh out my dayes in griefe,
   And as my beads count miseries,
My wound would meet with no reliefe,
   For all the balsome of mine eyes;
I'le therefore set my heart at rest,
And of bad market make the best.

Some set their hearts on winged wealth,
   Others to honour's towers aspire;
But give me freedom and my health,
   And there's the sum of my desire,
If all the world should pay me rent,
It could not add to my content.

There is no fence against our fate,
   Eve's daughters all are bound to sorrow,
Vicissitudes upon us wait,
   That laugh to-day, and lower to-morrow.
Why should we then with wrinkl'd care,
Deface what Nature made so fair?

SIR JOHN SUCKLING

Verses

I am confirm'd a woman can
Love this, or that, or any other man;
This day she's melting hot,
To-morrow swears she knows you not;
If she but a new object find,
Then straight she's of another mind.
    Then hang me, Ladies, at your door,
    If e'er I doat upon you more.

Yet still I love the fairsome (why?
For nothing but to please my eye);
And so the fat and soft-skinn'd dame
I'll flatter to appease my flame;
For she that's musical I'll long,
When I am sad, to sing a song.
    Then hang me, Ladies, at your door,
    If e'er I doat upon you more.

I'll give my fancy leave to range
Through everywhere to find out change;
The black, the brown, the fair shall be
But objects of variety,
I'll court you all to serve my turn,
But with such flames as shall not burn.
    Then hang me, Ladies, at your door,
    If e'er I doat upon you more.

A Poem with the Answer

1

Out upon it, I have lov'd
    Three whole days together;
And am like to love three more,
    If it prove fair weather.

2

Time shall moult away his wings,
    Ere he shall discover
In the whole wide world again
    Such a constant lover.

3

But the spite on't is, no praise
    Is due at all to me:
Love with me had made no stays,
    Had it any been but she.

4

Had it any been but she,
    And that very face,
There had been at least ere this
    A dozen dozen in her place.

Sir Toby Matthews' Reply

1

Say, but did you love so long?
    In troth, I needs must blame you:

Passion did your judgment wrong,
   Or want of reason shame you.

2

Truth, Time's fair and witty daughter,
   Shortly shall discover,
Y' are a subject fit for laughter,
   And more fool than lover.

3

But I grant you merit praise
   For your constant folly:
Since you doted three whole days,
   Were you not melancholy?

4

She to whom you prov'd so true,
   And that very very face,
Puts each minute such as you
   A dozen dozen to disgrace.

Proffered Love Rejected

It is not four years ago,
   I offered forty crowns
To lie with her a night or so:
   She answer'd me in frowns.

Not two years since, she meeting me
   Did whisper in my ear,
That she would at my service be,
   If I contented were.

I told her I was cold as snow,
   And had no great desire;
But should be well content to go
   To twenty, but no higher.

Some three months since or thereabout,
   She, that so coy had been,
Bethought herself and found me out,
   And was content to sin.

I smil'd at that, and told her I
   Did think it something late,
And that I'd not repentance buy
   At above half the rate.

This present morning early she
   Forsooth came to my bed,
And gratis there she offered me
   Her high-priz'd maidenhead.

I told her that I thought it then
   Far dearer than I did,
When I at first the forty crowns
   For one night's lodging bid.

Upon A. M.

Yield all, my love; but be withal as coy,
As if thou knews't not how to sport and toy:
The fort resign'd with ease, men cowards prove
And lazy grow. Let me besiege my love,
Let me despair at least three times a day,
And take repulses upon each essay;
If I but ask a kiss, straight blush as red

As if I tempted for thy maidenhead:
Contract thy smiles, if that they go too far,
And let thy frowns be such as threaten war:
That face which nature sure never intended
Should e'er be marr'd, because't could ne'er be mended.
Take no corruption from thy grandame Eve;
Rather want faith to save thee, than believe
Too soon; for credit me 'tis true,
Men most of all enjoy, when least they do.

The Careless Lover

1

Never believe me, if I love,
Or know what 'tis, or mean to prove;
And yet in faith I lie, I do,
And she's extremely handsome too;
    She's fair, she's wondrous fair,
    But I care not who know it,
    Ere I'll die for love, I'll fairly forego it.

2

This heat of hope, or cold of fear,
My foolish heart could never bear:
One sigh imprison'd ruins more
Than earthquakes have done heretofore:
    She's fair, etc.

3

When I am hungry, I do eat,
And cut no fingers 'stead of meat;

Nor with much gazing on her face
Do e'er rise hungry from the place:
   She's fair, etc.

4

A gentle round fill'd to the brink
To this and t'other friend I drink;
And when 'tis nam'd another's health,
I never make it hers by stealth:
   She's fair, etc.

5

Blackfriars to me, and old Whitehall,
Is even as much as is the fall
Of fountains on a pathless grove,
And nourishes as much my love:
   She's fair, etc.

6

I visit, talk, do business, play,
And for a need laugh out a day:
Who does not thus in Cupid's school,
He makes not love, but plays the fool:
   She's fair, etc.

Love and Debt alike Troublesome

This one request I make to him that sits the clouds above,
That I were freely out of debt, as I am out of love.
Then for to dance, to drink and sing, I should be very willing,
I should not owe one lass a kiss, nor ne'er a knave a shilling.
'Tis only being in love and debt that breaks us of our rest;
And he that is quite out of both, of all the world is blest:
He sees the golden age, wherein all things were free and common;

He eats, he drinks, he takes his rest, he fears no man nor woman.
Though Croesus compassed great wealth, yet he still craved more,
He was as needy a beggar still, as goes from door to door,
Though Ovid were a merry man, love ever kept him sad;
He was as far from happiness, as one that is stark mad.
Our merchant he in goods is rich, and full of gold and treasure;
But when he thinks upon his debts, that thought destroys his
    pleasure.
Our courtier thinks that he's preferr'd, whom every man envies;
When love so rumbles in his pate, no sleep comes in his eyes.
Our gallant's case is worse of all, he lies so just betwixt them;
For he's in love, and he's in debt, and knows not which most vex
    him.
But he that can eat beef, and feed on bread which is so brown
May satisfy his appetite, and owe no man a crown:
And he that is content with lasses clothed in plain woollen
May cool his heat in every place, he need not to be sullen,
Nor sigh for love of lady fair; for this each wise man knows
As good stuff under flannel lies, as under silken clothes.

('Tis Now, Since I Sat Down Before)

1

'Tis now, since I sat down before
    That foolish fort, a heart;
(Time, strangely spent) a year and more,
    And still I did my part:

2

Made my approaches, from her hand
    Unto her lip did rise,
And did already understand
    The language of her eyes;

3

Proceeded on with no less art,
  My tongue was engineer;
I thought to undermine the heart
  By whispering in the ear.

4

When this did nothing, I brought down
  Great cannon-oaths, and shot
A thousand thousand to the town,
  And still it yielded not.

5

I then resolved to starve the place
  By cutting off all kisses,
Praising and gazing on her face,
  And all such little blisses.

6

To draw her out, and from her strength
  I drew all batteries in:
And brought myself to lie at length
  As if no siege had been.

7

When I had done what man could do,
  And thought the place mine own,
The enemy lay quiet too,
  And smil'd at all was done.

8

I sent to know from whence and where
    These hopes and this relief?
A spy inform'd, Honour was there,
    And did command in chief.

9

March, march, quoth I, the word straight give,
    Let's lose no time, but leave her;
That giant upon air will live,
    And hold it out for ever.

10

To such a place our camp remove,
    As will no siege abide;
I hate a fool that starves her love,
    Only to feed her pride.

A Ballad upon a Wedding

I tell thee Dick where I have been,
Where I the rarest things have seen;
    Oh things without compare!
Such sights again cannot be found
In any place on English ground,
    Be it at Wake, or Fair.

At Charing Cross, hard by the way
Where we (thou know'st) do sell our Hay,
    There is a house with stairs;
And there did I see coming down
Such folk as are not in our Town,
    Vorty at least, in Pairs.

Amongst the rest, one Pest'lent fine,
(His beard no bigger though than thine)
   Walkst on before the rest:
Our Landlord looks like nothing to him:
The King (God bless him) 'twould undo him,
   Should he go still so drest.

At Course-a-Park, without all doubt,
He should have first been taken out
   By all the Maids i' th' Town:
Though lusty Roger there had been,
Or little George upon the Green,
   Or Vincent of the Crown.

But wot you what? the youth was going
To make an end of all his wooing;
   The parson for him staid:
Yet by his leave (for all his haste)
He did not so much wish all past
   (Perchance) as did the Maid.

The maid (and thereby hangs a tale)
For such a maid no Whitson-ale
   Could ever yet produce:
No Grape that's kindly ripe, could be
So round, so plump, so soft as she,
   Nor half so full of Juice.

Her finger was so small, the Ring
Would not stay on which they did bring;
   It was too wide a Peck:
And to say truth (for out it must)
It lookst like the great Collar (just)
   About our young Colts neck.

Her feet beneath her Petticoat,
Like little mice stole in and out,
 As if they fear'd the light:
But oh, she dances such a way!
No Sun upon an Easter-day,
 Is half so fine a sight.

He would have kiss'd her once or twice,
But she would not, she was so nice,
 She would not do 't in sight;
And then she lookt as who should say
I will do what I list to-day;
 And you shall do 't at night.

Her Cheeks so rare a white was on,
No Daisy makes comparison,
 (Who sees them is undone)
For streaks of red were mingled there,
Such as are on a Katherine Pear,
 (The side that's next the Sun).

Her lips were red, and one was thin,
Compar'd to that was next her chin,
 (Some bee had stung it newly.)
But, Dick, her eyes to guard her face,
I durst no more upon them gaze,
 Than on the Sun in July.

Her mouth so small when she does speak,
Thou'dst swear her teeth her words did break,
 That they might passage get,
But she so handled still the matter,
They came as geod as ours, or better,
 And are not spent a whit.

If wishing should be any sin,
The Parson himself had guilty been,
  (She lookt that day so purely:)
And, did the youth so oft the feat
At night, as some did in conceit,
  It would have spoil'd him, surely.

Passion oh me! how I run on!
There's that that would be thought upon,
  I trow; besides the Bride,
The bus'ness of the Kitchin's great,
For it is fit that men should eat;
  Nor was it there deny'd.

Just in the nick the Cook knock'd thrice,
And all the waiters in a trice
  His summons did obey,
Each serving-man with dish in hand,
March'd boldly up, like our Train'd Band,
  Presented, and away.

When all the meat was on the Table,
What man of knife, or teeth, was able
  To stay to be entreated?
And this the very reason was,
Before the Parson could say Grace,
  The Company was seated.

Now hats fly off, and youths carouse;
Healths first go round, and then the house,
  The Bride's came thick and thick:
And when 'twas nam'd another's health,
Perhaps he made it hers by stealth;
  (And who could help it, Dick?)

O'th'sudden up they rise and dance;
Then sit again, and sigh, and glance:
   Then dance again and kiss:
Thus sev'ral ways the time did pass,
Whilst ev'ry Woman wish'd her place,
   And ev'ry Man wished his.

By this time all were stol'n aside
To counsel and undress the Bride;
   But that he must not know:
But yet 'twas thought he guess'd her mind,
And did not mean to stay behind
   Above an hour or so.

When in he came, Dick, there she lay,
Like new-fall'n snow melting away,
   ('Twas time, I trow, to part):
Kisses were now the only stay,
Which soon she gave, as who would say,
   God B'w' ye, with all my heart.

But, just as Heav'ns would have to cross it,
In came the Bridemaids with the Posset:
   The bridegroom eat in spite;
For, had he left the Women to 't,
It would have cost two hours to do 't,
   Which were too much that night.

At length the candle's out, and now,
All that they had not done, they do:
   What that is, who can tell?
But I believe it was no more
Than thou and I have done before
   With Bridget, and with Nell.

NAHUM TATE

The Penance

Nymph Fanaret, the gentlest maid
That ever happy swain obeyed,
(For what offence I cannot say)
A day and night, and half a day,
Banished her shepherd from her sight;
His fault for certain was not slight,
Or sure this tender judge had ne'er
Imposed a penance so severe.
And lest she should anon revoke
What in her warmer rage she spoke,
She bound the sentence with an oath,
Protested by her faith and troth,
Nought should compound for his offence
But the full time of abstinence.
Yet when his penance-glass were run,
His hours of castigation done,
Should he defer one moment's space
To come and be restored to grace,
With sparkling threat'ning eyes she swore
That failing would incense her more
Than all his trespasses before.

JOHN TATHAM

The Letter

Goe, pale-fac't Paper, to my Deare,
And whisper this into her eare:
Though I absent am, yet shee
Keeping thee, embraces mee.
Let no rude hand dare to touch thee,
Care not though a thousand grutch thee
Of that blisse which in her Hive
Thou enjoy'st till I arrive,
And be sure thou dost not flye
From the glances of her eye.
Where she goes be thou about her,
Gad not thou abroad without her;
Nor let any dare to see
What's betweene my Love and thee.
Nay, and when she chance to sleepe,
Gently to her Bosome creepe,
Where, I charge thee, rest till she
With her kisses waken thee.
Goe and prosper for a space,
Till I rob thee of thy place.

Reason

Reason and I long time known friends,
   In all things did comply,
Till suddenly for unknown ends
   It shun'd my company.

And whatsoe're I said or did,
　　It still did fly the Sense,
As though some Sophistry lay hid,
　　Or Errour came from thence.

At last admiring at the Cause
　　Of its so strange Neglect,
I Conjur'd it by its own Laws,
　　To yield me more respect ;

And to resolve me speedily
　　Why we at difference were,
Since first a solemn League did tie
　　Us to a Sense more fair,
Knowing I was in Love, it answered me,
　　Reason and Madmen never could agree.

AURELIAN TOWNSHEND

Upon Kinde and True Love

'Tis not how witty, nor how free,
Nor yet how beautifull she be,
But how much kinde and true to me.
Freedom and Wit none can confine,
And Beauty like the Sun doth shine,
But kinde and true are only mine.

Let others with attention sit,
To listen, and admire her wit,
That is a rock where I'll not split.
Let others dote upon her eyes,
And burn their hearts for sacrifice,
Beauty's a calm where danger lyes.

But Kinde and True have been long tried
A harbour where we may confide,
And safely there at anchor ride.
From change of winds there we are free,
And need not feare Storme's tyrannie,
Nor Pirate, though a Prince he be.

EDMUND WALLER

Written in My Lady Speke's Singing-Book

Her fair eyes, if they could see
What themselves have wrought in me,
Would at least with pardon look
On this scribbling in her book:
If that she the writer scorn,
This may from the rest be torn,
With the ruin of a part,
But the image of her graces
Fills my heart and leaves no spaces.

Song

Chloris! farewell. I now must go;
For if with thee I longer stay,
Thy eyes prevail upon me so,
I shall prove blind, and lose my way.

Fame of thy beauty, and thy youth,
Among the rest, me hither brought;
Finding this fame fall short of truth,
Made me stay longer than I thought.

For I'm engaged by word and oath,
A servant to another's will;
Yet, for thy love, I'd forfeit both,
Could I be sure to keep it still.

But what assurance can I take,
When thou, foreknowing this abuse,

For some more worthy lover's sake,
Mayst leave me with so just excuse?

For thou mayst say, 'twas not thy fault
That thou didst thus inconstant prove;
Being by my example taught
To break thy oath, to mend thy love.

No, Chloris! no: I will return,
And raise thy story to that height,
That strangers shall at distance burn,
And she distrust me reprobate.

Then shall my love this doubt displace,
And gain such trust, that I may come
And banquet sometimes on thy face,
But make my constant meals at home.

Of English Verse

Poets may boast, as safely vain,
Their works shall with the world remain;
Both, bound together, live or die,
The verses and the prophecy.

But who can hope his lines should long
Last in a daily changing tongue?
While they are new, envy prevails;
And as that dies, our language fails.

When architects have done their part,
The matter may betray their art;
Time, if we use ill-chosen stone,
Soon brings a well-built palace down.

Poets that lasting marble seek,
Must carve in Latin, or in Greek;
We write in sand, our language grows,
And, like the tide, our work o'erflows.

Chaucer his sense can only boast;
The glory of his numbers lost!
Years have defaced his matchless strain;
And yet he did not sing in vain.

The beauties which adorned that age,
The shining subjects of his rage,
Hoping they should immortal prove,
Rewarded with success his love.

This was the generous poet's scope;
And all an English pen can hope,
To make the fair approve his flame,
That can so far extend their fame.

Verse, thus designed, has no ill fate,
If it arrive but at the date
Of fading beauty; if it prove
But as long-lived as present love.

Song

Say, lovely dream! where couldst thou find
Shades to counterfeit that face?
Colours of this glorious kind
Come not from any mortal place.

In heaven itself thou sure wert dressed
With that angel-like disguise:
Thus deluded am I blessed,
And see my joy with closed eyes.

But ah! this image is too kind
To be other than a dream;
Cruel Sacharissa's mind
Never put on that sweet extreme!

Fair dream! if thou intend'st me grace,
Change that heavenly face of thine;
Paint despised love in thy face,
And make it to appear like mine.

Pale, wan, and meagre let it look,
With a pity-moving shape,
Such as wander by the brook
Of Lethe, or from graves escape.

Then to that matchless numph appear,
In whose shape thou shinest so;
Softly in her sleeping ear,
With humble words, express my woe.

Perhaps from greatness, state, and pride,
Thus surprised she may fall;
Sleep does disproportion hide,
And, death resembling, equals all.

To Phyllis

Phyllis! why should we delay
Pleasures shorter than the day
Could we (which we never can)
Stretch our lives beyond their span,
Beauty like a shadow flies,
And our youth before us dies.
Or would youth and beauty stay,

Love hath wings, and will away.
Love hath swifter wings than Time;
Change in love to heaven does climb.
Gods, that never change their state,
Vary oft their love and hate.
　　Phyllis! to this truth we owe
All the love betwixt us two.
Let not you and I inquire
What has been our past desire;
On what shepherds you have smiled,
Or what nymphs I have beguiled;
Leave it to the planets too,
What we shall hereafter do;　·
For the joys we now may prove,
Take advice of present love.

The Selfe Banished

It is not that I love you less,
Than when before your feet I lay,
But to prevent the sad increase
Of hopeless love, I keep away.

In vaine (alas!) for everything
Which I have knowne belong to you,
Your forme does to my fancy bring,
And make my old wounds bleed anew.

Who in the Spring from the new Sun
Already has a Fever got,
Too late begins these shafts to shun
Which Phoebus through his veines has shot.

Too late he would the paine assuage,
And to thick shadowes does retire;

About with him he beares the rage,
And in his tainted blood the fire.

But vow'd I have, and never must
Your banish'd servant trouble you;
For if I breake, you may mistrust
The vow I made to love you too.

Song

Goe lovely Rose,
   Tell her that wastes her time and me,
    That now she knowes,
When I resemble her to thee,
    How sweet and fair she seems to be.

    Tell her that's young,
And shuns to have her graces spied,
    That hadst thou sprung
In deserts where no men abide,
    Thou must have uncommended died.

    Small is the worth
Of beauty from the light retir'd:
    Bid her come forth,
Suffer her selfe to be desir'd,
    And not blush so to be admir'd.

    Then die, that she
The common fate of all things rare
    May read in thee,
How small a part of time they share,
    That are so wondrous sweet and faire.

On a Girdle

That which her slender waist confin'd,
Shall now my joyfull temples bind;
No Monarch but would give his Crowne
His Armes might doe what this has done.

It is my Heavens extreamest Spheare,
The pale which held the lovely Deare,
My joy, my griefe, my hope, my Love,
Doe all within this Circle move.

A narrow compass, and yet there
Dwells all that's good, and all that's faire:
Give me but what this Ribbon ty'd,
Take all the sun goes round beside.

ROWLAND WATKYNS

The Wish

A little house, a quiet wife,
Sufficient food to nourish life,
Most perfect health, and free from harm,
Convenient clothes to keepe me warm.
The liberty of foot, and mind,
And grace the ways of God to find.
This is the summe of my desire,
Until I come unto heaven's quire.

ANNE WHARTON

(Spite of Thy Godhead, Powerful Love)

Spite of thy godhead, powerful Love,
    I will my torments hide;
But what avail if life must prove
    A sacrifice to pride?

Pride, thou'rt become my goddess now,
    To thee I'll altars rear,
To thee each morning pay my vow
    And offer every tear.

But oh, I fear, should Philemon
    Once take thy injured part,
I should soon cast that idol down,
    And offer him my heart.

(How Hardly I Conceal'd My Tears)

How hardly I conceal'd my tears!
    How oft did I complain!
When many tedious days my fears
    Told me I lov'd in vain.

But now my joys as wild are grown,
    And hard to be conceal'd:
Sorrow may make a silent moan,
    But joy will be reveal'd.

I tell it to the bleating flocks,
    To every stream and tree,

And bless the hollow murmuring rocks
    For echoing back to me.

Thus you may see with how much joy
    We what we wish, believe;
'Tis hard such passion to destroy,
    But easy to deceive.

BIOGRAPHICAL NOTES

PHILIP AYRES (1638–1712) was educated at Westminster School and St John's College, Oxford. He was a friend of Dryden's. His LYRIC POEMS were published in 1687. His EMBLEMATA appeared earlier, but the date of publication is uncertain.

THOMAS BEEDOME (d. 1640?) was the author of one posthumous collection of verses, POEMS, DIVINE AND HUMANE (1641). Many of the poems were pirated by Henry Bold in 1657. The only modern edition of Beedome is a selection edited by Francis Meynell and published in an edition of 1250 copies by the Nonesuch Press in 1928.

APHRA BEHN (1640–1689) was born at Wye in Kent, the daughter of John Johnson, a barber. She married a Dutch merchant named Behn and after his death worked as a British spy in Antwerp. She wrote many plays, including THE FORC'D MARRIAGE (1671), THE DUTCH LOVER (1673), OROONOKO (1678), ABDELAZAR (1677), and THE TOWN FOP (1677). Her poems were published in 1684.

ALEXANDER BROME (1620–1666) was an attorney. His comedy, THE CUNNING LOVERS, was first acted at Drury Lane in 1651 and published in 1654. His POEMS first appeared in 1661. A larger second edition appeared in 1664.

WILLIAM BROWNE (1592–1643?) was born in Tavistock, Devon, and educated at Exeter College, Oxford, and, as a young man, practiced law. In about 1624 he returned to Exeter College from the Inner Temple to act as tutor to the Earl of Caernarvon, and received his M.A. He was later in the service of the Earl of Pembroke. His BRITANNIA'S PASTORALS were published in two parts, the first in 1613 and the second in 1616, both being reprinted in 1625. THE SHEPHERD'S PIPE was published in 1614. His later poems remained in manuscript during his lifetime. The best available edition of his work is that in *The Muse's Library*.

GEORGE VILLIERS, THE SECOND DUKE OF BUCKINGHAM (1627–1688) was born in London, and became one of the most prominent courtiers and politicians of the reign of Charles II. He was killed at the battle of Kirby Moorside on 17 April 1688. His collected works were published in 1704.

JOHN BUNYAN (1628–1688) was born at Elstow, near Bedford, and was the son of a tinker. After serving as a soldier he became a dissenting preacher and spent the greater part of the years 1660–1672 in prison. In 1672 he was released and became pastor of a congregation in Bedford. In 1675 he was again imprisoned, and during his confinement wrote THE PILGRIM'S PROGRESS, which was published in 1678. He was the author of numerous books, the most significant being THE PILGRIM'S PROGRESS (1678), THE LIFE AND DEATH OF MR. BADMAN (1680) and THE HOLY WAR (1682).

THOMAS CAREW (1595?–1639?), the son of a lawyer, was educated at Merton College, Oxford, gaining his B.A. in 1611. He lived in the Middle Temple for a time in 1612 and from 1613 to 1615 was a secretary to Sir Dudley Carleton, the ambassador to Italy. He was a great favourite with Charles I, and noted for his dissipation. In 1619 he visited France with Lord Herbert of Cherbury. His masque, COELUM BRITANNICUM, was performed in the Banqueting Hall in Whitehall on 18 February, 1633 and published the following year. He died in 1639 and his poems were published in 1640, other and enlarged editions appearing in 1653, 1651, and 1671. The best recent edition of his work is that edited by R. Dunlap (Oxford University Press, 1949).

WILLIAM CARTWRIGHT (1611–1643) was educated at Westminster and Christ Church, Oxford, and was the author of many plays, and took holy orders in 1638. He was noted as a preacher at Oxford and in Salisbury where he became the Succentor of the Cathedral. In 1642 he was appointed Reader in Metaphysic to the University of Oxford. He was imprisoned by the Cromwellians for a short while, but released when Charles I made Oxford his headquarters. He was appointed Junior Proctor to the University in 1643 but died of a fever later in the year. He contributed poems to many of the miscellanies of the period and was himself the author of THE ROYALL SLAVE (1639), TO THE RIGHT HONOURABLE PHILIP EARLE OF PEMBROKE (1641), COMEDIES, TRAGI-COMEDIES, WITH OTHER POEMS (1651), AN OFF-SPRING OF MERCY (1652), and NOVEMBER, OR, SIGNAL DAYS (1671). The definitive edition of his PLAYS AND POEMS is that of G. Blakemore Evans (The University of Wisconsin Press, 1951).

ROBERT CHAMBERLAIN (1607–1663?) wrote a number of collections of poems and epigrams, several broadsides and pamphlets, a comedy, THE SWAGGERING DAMSEL (1640) and a collection of verse, NOCTURNALL LUCUBRATIONS (1638, reissued 1652). There is no modern edition of his work.

SIR JAMES CHAMBERLAYNE (1640–1699) was the author of two books of religious verse, A SACRED POEM (1680) and MANU-DUCTIO AD COELUM (1681). There is no modern edition of his work.

JOHN CLEVELAND (1613-1658) was born at Loughborough, the son of a clergyman. He studied at Christ's College, Cambridge, and in 1634 became a Fellow of St. John's. He served with the Royalist forces during the Civil War. His poems first appeared in 1647, and were reissued eight times during the year. Many other editions followed before the WORKS OF MR. JOHN CLEVELAND appeared in 1687. The best available edition of Cleveland's poems is that by Brian Morris and Eleanor Withington from The Clarendon Press (1967).

SIR ASTON COKAYNE (1608–1684) wrote a number of plays, the most popular being TRAPPOLIN, A SUPPOSED PRINCE (1658). His SMALL POEMS OF DIVERS SORTS was published in 1658 and reissued under various titles several times.

MATTHEW COPPINGER (fl. 1682) published one book, POEMS, SONGS AND LOVE-VERSES (1682) which has never been reprinted. Nothing is known of his life.

CHARLES COTTON (1630–1687) was born at Beresford, Staffordshire. Though chiefly famous for his contributions to Izaak Walton's THE COMPLEAT ANGLER, he must also be remembered as the translator of Montaigne's ESSAYS (1685). He was the author of a number of other translations and minor works. His POEMS first appeared posthumously in 1689. The best modern edition is that by John Buxton in *The Muse's Library*.

ABRAHAM COWLEY (1618–1667) was born in London, the son of a stationer, and educated at Westminster School and Cambridge. He joined Queen Henrietta Maria in exile in 1646, and served as a courier carrying messages from France to England. He returned to England in 1656 and lived at Chertsey. His juvenile POETICAL BLOSSOMS was published in 1633. His pastoral drama LOVE'S RIDDLE appeared in 1638, and was followed by two collections of poems, THE MISTRESS (1647) and MISCELLANIES (1656). His COLLECTED WORKS were first published in 1669. The only available modern edition is the 1906 one by A. R. Waller for the Cambridge University Press.

RICHARD CRASHAW (1613?–1649) was born in London, the son of a clergyman, and educated at Charterhouse and Pembroke College, in 1644, and in 1649 was appointed a sub-canon of the Basilica Church of Our Lady of Loretto in Italy, but died there shortly after arriving to take up his post. His religious poems STEPS TO THE TEMPLE and his secular poems THE DELIGHTS OF THE MUSE were published together in one volume in 1646. A modern edition of his Poems is that by L. C. Martin for the Oxford English Texts series (2nd ed. 1957).

JOHN CUTTS, BARON CUTTS OF GOWRAN (1661–1707) was born in Dublin and served as a professional soldier. He came to England with William of Orange in 1688. He fought at the Battle of the Boyne (1690), was wounded at the Siege of Limerick, and nicknamed 'Salamander' for his bravery under fire during the Siege of Namur (1695). He accompanied Marlborough to Holland in 1701 and was third in command at the Battle of Blenheim. He was later appointed Commander in

Chief of Ireland. His POETICAL EXERCISES were published in 1687.

JOHN DANCER (fl. 1660) was a dramatist who worked with the Theatre Royal, Dublin. His works include AMINTA (1660), NICOMEDE (1671), THE COMPARISON OF PLATO AND ARISTOTLE (1673), and a play, AGRIPPA (1675).

GEORGE DANIEL (1616–1657) published nothing in his lifetime. His poems were edited from the manuscripts by A. B. Grosart in 1878.

SIR WILLIAM DAVENANT (or D'AVENANT) (1606–1668) was born in Oxford, the son of an innkeeper. About the year 1620 he entered the service of the Duchess of Richmond as a page, and later served as page to Fulke Greville, Lord Brooke. He began writing plays in the late 1620's and was made Poet Laureate in 1638. He was several times imprisoned for political reasons, but after the Restoration achieved security and was in favour at court. Among his plays are: ALBOVINE (1629), THE CRUEL BROTHER (1630), THE PLATONIC LOVERS (1636), THE WITS (1636), LOVE AND HONOUR (1649), and THE RIVALS (1664). He produced reworked versions of Shakespeare's TEMPEST, MACBETH, and JULIUS CAESAR, and was the author of the first English Opera THE SIEGE OF RHODES (1656). It is believed that this gave rise to the first appearance of a woman upon the English stage. Apart from the songs in his plays, Davenant's main achievement in non-dramatic poetry was his epic, GONDIBERT (1651).

CHARLES SACKVILLE, EARL OF DORSET (1637–1706) was privately educated and travelled abroad until the Restoration when he returned to England and became a Member of Parliament for East Grinstead. He served under the Duke of York in the Dutch War in 1665 and became a Gentleman of the Bedchamber and one of the King's favourites. He was Lord Chamberlain of the Household under King William and in 1691 was dubbed a Knight of the Garter. Though some of his poems appeared in a number of miscellanies during his lifetime, his WORKS were not published until 1749.

JOHN DRYDEN (1631–1700) was born in Aldwinkle, Northamptonshire, the son of a clergyman, and educated at Westminster School and Trinity College, Cambridge. Originally of the Puritan party, he went over to the Royalist cause on the Restoration of Charles II. His early work was in poetry. His HEROIC STANZAS on the death of Cromwell appeared in 1659, and his ASTREA REDUX, celebrating the Restoration, appeared in 1660. He became a Fellow of the Royal Society in 1662, and the following year married Lady Elizabeth Howard. From this time onwards he made his living as a playwright, producing over twenty comedies, heroic tragedies, adaptations, translations, and opera. His best known plays are THE INDIAN EMPEROR (1665), THE CONQUEST OF GRANADA (1670), AURANGZEBE (1675), ALL FOR LOVE (1678), MARRIAGE-A-LA-MODE (1673) and THE SPANISH FRYAR (1681). He was the author of many critical essays including the important AN ESSAY OF DRAMATIC POESY (1668), and he produced translations of Virgil and Juvenal. His most important poems are ANNUS MIRABILIS (1667), ABSALOM AND ACHITOPHEL (1681–1682), THE MEDALL (1682), MACFLECKNOE (1682), THE HIND AND THE PANTHER (1687), this last being written shortly after his conversion to Roman Catholicism. He succeeded Sir William Davenant as Poet Laureate in 1668, and in 1670 became Historiographer Royal, but lost both these positions at the Revolution of 1688, being succeeded by Thomas Shadwell, whom he had ridiculed in MACFLECKNOE. He was buried in Westminster Abbey.

THOMAS DUFFETT (fl. 1678) was both a playwright and poet. His collection of poems is NEW POEMS, SONGS, PROLOGUES AND EPILOGUES, SET BY THE MOST EMINENT MUSICIANS ABOUT THE TOWN (1676).

THOMAS D'URFEY (1653?–1723) was born in Devonshire, and but little is known of his life until 1676 when his first play THE

SIEGE OF MEMPHIS was produced. In November 1676 his second play, a comedy, MADAM FICKLE, was produced and much applauded by the King. From that time onwards Tom D'Urfey became one of the King's favourite entertainers and companions, and though he continued to produce a large number of mediocre plays, his reputation rested mainly upon his songs which were popular with both the Court and the general public. These songs were published in many collections, the most comprehensive being the two volumes of WIT AND MIRTH: or PILLS TO PURGE MELANCHOLY (1719). An excellent selection of D'Urfey's songs is that edited by Cyrus Lawrence Day for Harvard University Press in 1933.

'EPHELIA' (fl. 1679) remains a mystery. Her FEMALE POEMS ON SEVERAL OCCASIONS was published in 1679 and reprinted with additions in 1682.

SIR GEORGE ETHEREGE (1635?–1691) was Charles II's ambassador at The Hague and, later, James II's representative at Ratisbon. He retired to Paris in 1888 in some disgrace for his breaches of etiquette and his debauchery. He wrote three comedies of intrigue, THE COMICAL REVENGE, OR LOVE IN A TUB (1664), SHE WOULD IF SHE COULD (1668), and THE MAN OF MODE, OR SIR FOPLING FLUTTER (1676). His POEMS were first adequately edited by James Thorpe for Princeton University Press in 1963.

MILDMAY FANE, THE SECOND EARL OF WESTMORELAND (1602–1665) fought for the Royalist cause and was afterwards Lord Lieutenant of Northamptonshire. He was the author of one book, OTIA SACRA (1648).

SIR RICHARD FANSHAWE (1608–1666) was born at Ware Park, Hertfordshire and in 1635 he became secretary to Lord Aston, the Ambassador to Spain. He joined King Charles's forces at Oxford when the Civil War began, and was captured at the Battle of Worcester (1651). After the Restoration he was appointed Ambassador to Portugal (1661) and then Ambassador to Spain (1664). His most important work is his translation of Camoens THE LUSIAD which appeared in 1655. He died in Madrid. There is a modern (1964) edition of his shorter poems and the translation by N. W. Bawcutt for the Liverpool University Press.

OWEN FELLTHAM (1602?–1668) lived in Northamptonshire. His RESOLVES: DIVINE, MORALL, POLITICALL, a collection of a hundred short essays, was published in 1620 and frequently reprinted. The 1661 edition contained thirty-nine poems under the heading LUSORIA, OR OCCASIONAL PIECES.

THOMAS FLATMAN (1637–1688) was born in London and educated at the Universities of Oxford and Cambridge. Although a lawyer by profession, he became renowned as a painter of miniatures, as well as a poet. He became a Fellow of the Royal Society in 1668. His POEMS were first published in 1674, and were republished, with additions, four times before his death. The best available text is that in George Saintsbury's MINOR POETS OF THE CAROLINE PERIOD, Volume III (1921, reprinted 1968).

SIDNEY GODOLPHIN (1610–1643) was born in Godolphin, Cornwall, the son of Sir William Godolphin, and educated at Exeter College, Oxford. He became a member of parliament for Helston in 1628 and served under Hopton at the very beginning of the Civil War. He was killed at Chagford in a skirmish on 10 February, 1643. The majority of his poems remained in manuscript until 1906 when they were published by George Saintsbury in Volume II of MINOR POETS OF THE CAROLINE PERIOD, and this remains the best available text.

ROBERT GOULD (1660?–1709?) published LOVE GIVEN O'RE, a popular satire against women, in 1683. His POEMS, CHIEFLY CONSISTING OF SATYRS AND SATYRICAL EPISTLES appeared in 1689.

WILLIAM HABINGTON (1605–1654) was born in Hindlip, Worcestershire and educated by Jesuits in France. He was the author of two historical works, THE HISTORY OF EDWARD IV (1640) and OBSERVATIONS UPON HISTORY (1641) and a play, THE QUEEN OF ARRAGON (1640). He is chiefly remembered, however, for his collection of lyrics, CASTARA, which was published in 1634. His POEMS were edited by Kenneth Allott in 1948.

ROBERT HEATH (fl. 1650) is known only as the author of a collection of poems, CLARASTELLA, published in 1650.

ROBERT HERRICK (1591–1674) was the son of a goldsmith, and educated at the University of Cambridge at both St. John's College and Trinity Hall. He was ordained priest and deacon at Peterborough in 1623. In 1627 he was a Chaplain in the Duke of Buckingham's army. On its return in 1628 he was given the vicarage of Dean Prior in Devonshire where he settled in 1630. He was deprived of his living by Parliament in 1647 but returned to it at the Restoration. His collected poems, HESPERIDES, were published in 1648. The definitive edition is that by L. C. Martin (The Clarendon Press, 1956).

THOMAS HEYRICK (1649–1694) was a Curate in Market Harborough, Leicestershire. His MISCELLANY POEMS were published in 1691.

SIR ROBERT HOWARD (1626–1698) was a Member of Parliament and Auditor of the Exchequer, and was caricatured as Sir Positive-at-all in Shadwell's 'The Sullen Lovers' (1668). He was allotted a voice in Dryden's prose dialogue Essay on Dramatic Poesy, and was well known as a playwright. His POEMS appeared in 1660.

PATHERICKE JENKYN (1639–1661?) published his only volume of verse in 1661. This was AMOREA, THE LOST LOVER . . . BEING POEMS, SONGS, ODES, PASTORALS, ELEGIES, LYRICK POEMS AND EPIGRAMS.

HENRY KING (1592–1669) was born in Buckinghamshire, the son of John King, Prebendary of St. Paul's who later became Bishop of London, and educated at Westminster School and

Christ Church, Oxford. He became Bishop of Chichester in 1642, and was ejected from his palace and position by Waller's soldiers at the surrender of the city to the Parliamentarian Army in 1643. He was restored to his Bishopric at the Restoration. His POEMS, ELEGIES, PARADOXES, AND SONNETS were published in 1657. The most reliable recent text is THE POEMS OF HENRY KING, edited by Margaret Crum, The Clarendon Press, 1965.

SIR FRANCIS KYNASTON (1587–1642) was born at Oteley in Shropshire, and educated at Oriel College, Oxford, and Trinity College, Cambridge. He was knighted in 1618, and was a Member of Parliament for Shropshire from 1621. His masque CORONA MINERVAE was published in 1635, and his long poem LEOLINE AND SYDANIS and his shorter CYNTHIADES OR AMOUROUS SONNETS were published together in one volume in 1642. He also translated the first book of Chaucer's Troilus and Cressida into Latin Rhyme-royal. His poems can be found in Volume II of George Saintsbury's MINOR POETS OF THE CAROLINE PERIOD (1906, reprinted 1968).

RICHARD LEIGH (1649?, alive in 1675) published one collection of poems, POEMS UPON SEVERAL OCCASIONS, AND TO SEVERAL PERSONS (1675).

RICHARD LOVELACE (1618?–1657) was educated at Charterhouse and Gloucester Hall, Oxford, gaining his M.A. in 1636. He took part in the Scottish expedition in 1639, and in 1642 was imprisoned for supporting the 'Kentish Petition'. In 1645 he joined Charles I at Oxford to fight for the Royalists. He was present at the Siege of Dunkirk in 1646, and was imprisoned in 1648. He was released in 1649 and died in poverty in 1657. His LUCASTA, EPODES, ODES, SONNETS, SONGS, and to which is added AMARANTHEA, A PASTORAL, was published in 1649. LUCASTA: POSTHUME POEMS appeared in 1659. The definitive edition of his poems is that by C. W. Wilkinson (Oxford University Press, 1930).

ANDREW MARVELL (1621–1678) was born in Holderness, East Yorkshire, the son of a clergyman, and educated at Hull Grammar School and Trinity College, Cambridge. He travelled abroad during the years 1642–1646. In 1650 he wrote his HORATIAN ODE UPON CROMWELL'S RETURN FROM IRELAND. He tutored General Fairfax's daughter in the years 1651–1653, when he became tutor to William Dutton, Cromwell's ward. In 1657 he assisted John Milton in his work as Latin Secretary to the Government. He was a Member of Parliament for Hull from 1659 till his death. He was the author of a number of satirical poems which were not printed until after his death. His MISCELLANEOUS POEMS were published in 1681. The best modern edition of his poems is that by H. M. Margoliouth for The Clarendon Press (1927).

JOHN MILTON (1608–1674) was born in London, the son of a scrivener, and educated at St. Paul's School and Christ's College, Cambridge. While still at the University he wrote ODE ON THE MORNING OF CHRIST'S NATIVITY (1629) and a number of other poems. He retired to Horton, Buckinghamshire in 1632 and remained there until 1638. During these years he wrote L'ALLEGRO, IL PENSEROSO, LYCIDAS and the masque, COMUS, which was produced by Henry Lawed at Ludlow Castle in 1634. In 1638–39 he travelled in Europe. On his return to England he wrote prose essays and tracts in the Puritan cause, and became in 1649 Latin Secretary to Cromwell. His prose works include AREOPAGITICA (1644), THE DOCTRINE AND DISCIPLINE OF DIVORCE (1643), OF THE TENURE OF KINGS AND MAGISTRATES (1649). In 1652 he became completely blind. His great religious epic, PARADISE LOST, was published in 1667, and PARADISE REGAINED and SAMSON AGONISTES appeared in 1671. Although prosecuted for his political activities at the Restoration, he escaped with nominal imprisonment, and retired from public life.

MARY MOLLINEUX (1648–1695) was the author of one book of poems, FRUITS OF RETIREMENT (1702).

JAMES GRAHAM, FIRST MARQUIS OF MONTROSE (1612–1650) was born in Montrose, Scotland, and educated at St. Andrews University. He fought with the Scottish Covenanters at the beginning of the Civil War but later joined the King by whom he was made Lieutenant General of Scotland in 1644. After many military successes against the Covenanters he was defeated at the battle of Philiphaugh in 1645 and banished from Scotland. He served Ferdinand III, the Holy Roman Emperor, as a Field Marshal. In 1650 he returned to Scotland but the Royalist rising he planned did not succeed. He was hanged at Edinburgh on 21 May, 1650. His poems were published in various collections after his death. His POEMS were edited by J. L. Weir in 1938.

JOHN NORRIS (1657–1711) was a Fellow of All Souls and a clergyman in Somerset. His POEMS AND DISCOVERIES appeared in 1684 and his A COLLECTION OF MISCELLANIES ETC. in 1687.

KATHERINE PHILIPS (1631–1664) was born in London, and became known as the 'matchless Orinda' because she had used the name in correspondence with Sir Charles Cotterel (Poliarchus). She translated Horace and Corneille, and these works were published together with her lyrics in the volume POEMS (1667).

SAMUEL PORDAGE (1633–1691?) was the son of John Pordage the astrologer. His books of verse are: POEMS UPON SEVERAL OCCASIONS (1660), AZARIA AND HUSHAI (1682), MUNDORUM EXPLICATIO (1661), THE MEDAL REVERS'D ETC. (1682). He is caricatured as 'Lame Mephibosheth, the wizard's son' in the second part of ABSALOM AND ACHITOPHEL.

JOHN WILMOT, EARL OF ROCHESTER (1647–1680) was born in Ditchley, Oxfordshire, and educated at Burford, and Wadham College, Oxford. In the years 1661–65 he travelled on the continent and studied at Padua. In 1665 he fought in the Dutch war and became, thereafter, a favourite of Charles II, by whom he was often banished from court and as often recalled. A notorious rake, and the writer of many risqué verses and satires, he died at Woodstock at the age of 33. His works were first published in 1691. The best modern edition of his poems is that by V. de S. Pinto (1953).

WENTWORTH DILLON, EARL OF ROSCOMMON (1633–1685) was born in Ireland and educated at the University of Caen. On leaving Caen he travelled into Italy and lived in Rome. He returned to England at the Restoration and was made Captain of the Band of Pensioners. He was Captain of the Guards in Dublin under the Duke of Ormonde for a period, and then Master of the Horse to the Duchess of York. He published a blank verse translation of Horace's ART OF POETRY (1680) and an ESSAY ON TRANSLATED VERSE (1684) as well as many verse translations and paraphrases of psalms and prayers. His POEMS were published in 1717.

SIR CHARLES SEDLEY (1639?–1701) was born in Kent, and became a Member of Parliament for New Romney. He wrote a number of plays, including, THE MULBERRY GARDEN (1668), ANTONY AND CLEOPATRA (1677), BELLAMIRE (1677), BEAUTY THE CONQUEROR (1702), and THE TYRANT KING OF CRETE (1702). His poems were included in his MISCELLANEOUS WORKS (1702). He was a member of the group of rakes which gathered at the court of Charles II.

SIR EDWARD SHERBURNE (1618–1702) was born in Oxford and educated privately, in England and abroad. In 1641 he succeeded his father as Clerk of His Majesty's Ordinance, but was ejected from the post by Parliament in 1642. He served the King at Oxford until the city fell to the Parliamentarians in 1646 when he went to live in London. In 1648 he published a translation of Seneca's MEDEA, and in 1651 his POEMS AND TRANS-LATIONS. On the Restoration he regained his post as Clerk of the Ordinance. He was knighted in 1682. In 1679 he published a translation of Seneca's TROADES OR THE ROYAL CAPTIVES.

JAMES SHIRLEY (1596–1666) was born in London and, although ordained, gave up his living and turned playwright. Between 1625 and 1642 he wrote well over thirty plays including THE WITTY FAIR ONE (1633), THE MAID'S REVENGE (1639), THE TRAITOR (1631), LOVE'S CRUELTY (1631), THE LADY OF PLEASURE (1635) and ST. PATRICK FOR IRELAND (1640). He also wrote a book of grammar for children which was published in 1660. After the theatres were closed in 1642 he made his living as a schoolmaster. He died during the Great Fire of London.

THOMAS STANLEY (1625–1678) was born in Hertfordshire. He was the author of a HISTORY OF PHILOSOPHY (1655–1662), and of POEMS AND TRANSLATIONS (1647) which achieved a second edition in 1651. The most reliable text is THE POEMS AND TRANSLATIONS OF THOMAS STANLEY, edited by Galbraith Miller Crump (Clarendon Press 1962).

MATTHEW STEVENSON (fl. 1654–1685) was the author of four books, OCCASION'S OFFSPRING (1664), THE TWELVE MONTHS (1661), POEMS (1665), and POEMS, OR A MISCELLANY (1673).

SIR JOHN SUCKLING (1609–1642) was educated at Trinity College, Cambridge. As a young man he travelled on the continent and served in the army of Gustavus Adolphus, returning to England in 1632 to become well known at court as a wit and rake. He took part in the expedition against Scotland in 1639. In 1641 he was a member of the conspiracy to free the Earl of Strafford, and was obliged, when the plot was discovered, to escape to France where he died in 1642. His published works are: AGLAURA (1638), THE DISCONTENTED COLONEL (1640), A COPY OF A LETTER WRITTEN TO THE LOWER HOUSE OF PARLIAMENT (1641), and FRAGMENTEA AUREA, A COLLECTION OF ALL THE INCOMPARABLE PIECES WRITTEN BY JOHN SUCKLING (1646). His Collected Works first appeared in 1676. The most reliable recent text is THE WORKS OF SIR JOHN SUCKLING IN PROSE AND VERSE, edited by A. Hamilton Thompson, Routledge (1910).

NAHUM TATE (1652–1715) was born in Dublin and educated at Trinity College, Dublin. His first volume of POEMS appeared in 1677 and his ESSAY ON PSALMODY in 1710. With Nicholas Brady, he produced a poetic version of the Psalms in 1696 and wrote, with Dryden, the second part of ABSALOM AND ACHITOPHEL (1682). He became Poet Laureate in 1692.

JOHN TATHAM (fl. 1632–1664) was the author of two books of verse, THE FANCIES' THEATER (1640) and OSTELLA: OR THE FACTION OF LOVE AND BEAUTY RECONCIL'D (1650).

AURELIAN TOWNSHEND (c. 1583–1643) was a friend of Ben Jonson, Thomas Carew, and Lord Herbert of Cherbury. He succeeded Ben Jonson as writer of Masques to the Court. He edited Carew's POEMS (1640).

EDMUND WALLER (1606–1687) was educated at Eton and Kings College, Cambridge. He was a favourite of the King and a Member of Parliament for many years, first entering the House in 1621 when he was only 16. He was arrested and imprisoned by the Parliament for conspiracy in 1643, but, by giving evidence against his companions, he escaped hanging and was merely fined and banished. He returned to England in 1652, and wrote a panegyric on Oliver Cromwell as well as a poem in praise of Charles II on his Restoration. He became a Member of Parliament again in 1661, and died in 1687. His published works are: SPEECH AGAINST PRELATES INNOVATIONS (1641), MR. WALLER'S SPEECH IN THE PAINTED CHAMBER (1641), SPEECH 4 JULY 1643 (1643), POEMS (1645; reprinted in 1664, 1668, 1682), A PANEGYRICK TO MY LORD PROTECTOR (1655), UPON THE LATE STORME, AND OF THE DEATH OF HIS HIGHNESSE (1658), THE KING, UPON HIS . . . HAPPY RETURN (1660), TO MY LADY MORTON (1661), A POEM IN ST. JAMES'S PARK (1661), UPON HER MAJESTY'S NEW BUILDINGS (1665), OF THE LADY MARY (1679), DIVINE POEMS (1685), THE MAID'S TRAGEDY, ALTER'D (1690), THE SECOND PART OF MR. WALLER'S POEMS (1690). The best edition of Waller's POEMS is that edited for the Muse's Library by G. Thorn-Drury in 1893.

ROWLAND WATKYNS (fl. 1635–1662?) was born in Longtown, Herefordshire, and became the vicar of Llanfrynach in Brecknockshire in 1635. He was dispossessed of his living by Cromwell in 1648, but reinstated at the Restoration. His one book of poems, FLAMMA SINE FUMO, was published in 1662.

ANNE WHARTON (1659–1685) was the author of two collections of poems, VINCULUM SOCIETATIS (1687) and A COLLECTION OF POEMS (1693). Her work also appeared in Dryden's MISCELLANY POEMS of 1684.

INDEX OF FIRST LINES